Dave Spence
403-875-9262

HELP!
I'm Barking
and I Can't be Quiet

by Daniel Q. Estep, Ph.D.
and Suzanne Hetts, Ph.D.

First published in 2004 by
Island Dog Press, Inc.
Updated edition published 2006 by Island Dog Press, Inc.
4994 S. Independence Way
Littleton, Colorado 80123

ISBN 0-9749542-3-3

Library of Congress Control Number: 2004095822

Dedication

This book is dedicated to our late friend, companion, and sweet-est boy, Mocha. We know you are running through fields, sniffing all the flowers, hanging out with your girlfriends Emma and Brie, and have an unlimited supply of pizza crusts.

Table of Contents

Acknowledgments

We would like to thank several people whose help was an integral part of completing this book. Barbara Munson for her editing; Dr. Stephen Zawistowski of the American Society for the Prevention of Cruelty to Animals for use of the drawings of the dog body postures; and Shannon Parish for her wonderful drawings of barking dogs that appear throughout the text. We owe a great debt of gratitude to our graphic artist and book designer, Kristi Endelicato of Metagraphics for bearing with us through all our changes and producing a great looking book.

Thanks, too, to Paul Miller and Darlene Larsen for reviewing and commenting on early drafts of the book, and Nancy Williams and Lori Holmberg for reviewing the revision. Their suggestions were valuable and improved the book.

Thanks to Joylise Hansen and Mogley (our cover dog).

Cover design and photo by Kristi Endelicato, Metagraphics.

About the Authors

Daniel Q. Estep, Ph.D. Applied Animal Behaviorist

Daniel Q. Estep holds a doctorate in psychology with a specialization in animal behavior from the University of Florida. He is certified by the Animal Behavior Society as an applied animal behaviorist.

Dr. Estep is internationally respected as a teacher, researcher, and lecturer in animal behavior. He regularly consults with veterinarians, pet professionals, humane organizations, government agencies and attorneys about animal behavior. He has published a variety of research papers and books as well as numerous articles for pet owners. He is coauthor of *Raising a Behaviorally Healthy Puppy: A Pet Parenting Guide* and numerous video and audio training programs for pet professionals and pet parents.

Suzanne Hetts, Ph.D. Applied Animal Behaviorist

Suzanne Hetts holds a doctorate in animal behavior from Colorado State University. She is certified by the Animal Behavior Society as an applied animal behaviorist.

Dr. Hetts has helped thousands of pet parents to improve their pets' behavior and relationships. She is often called upon to consult with animal professionals, veterinarians, dog trainers, humane societies and personal injury attorneys to help them understand and work with animal issues.

Dr. Hetts is a popular, award-winning international speaker, and author of *Pet Behavior Protocols: What to Say, What to Do, When to Refer,* published by AAHA Press and coauthor of *Raising a Behaviorally Healthy Puppy: A Pet Parenting Guide,* published by Island Dog Press, Inc. She directed the Delta Society's *Professional Standards for Dog Trainers* project and consults with major corporations in the pet industry. Her publications and videos are used in nationwide training programs for animal caretakers and pet parents.

Drs. Estep and Hetts own Animal Behavior Associates, Inc., a pet behavior consulting firm in Littleton, Colorado. Their firm provides professional animal consulting services to organizations and pet owners throughout North America and the world. They maintain a popular and active Web site (**www.AnimalBehaviorAssociates.com**) which contains a wealth of information for pet parents and pet professionals. Their Web site specific to barking problems is **www.BarkingHelp.com**. They share their home and their lives with Buffett the cat, Dalmatian Ashley and Irish Setter Coral.

Chapter One
Introduction

Does this sound familiar?

Do you feel as though your dog's barking makes greeting someone at the door impossible? You may have resorted to putting your dog outside or in another room when company arrives because your greeting can't be heard over your dog's ear-splitting welcome.

Does your dog's continual "on-patrol" behavior constantly startle you, as she barks at the sound of your neighbor's car door, passersby or the kids playing down the street? Do your admonishments to "BE QUIET!" fall on deaf ears?

Is your dog's barking a problem in other places, such as training classes, doggie day care or when she's boarded?

Have you returned home and found citations from Animal Control or nasty notes from neighbors about your noisy canine?

Perhaps you're not even sure your dog is barking too much—maybe you think you just have overly sensitive neighbors. If the complaining neighbor is someone you've had other, non-dog disputes with, your dog's barking may just be adding fuel to the fire. Animal control officers find that many barking dog complaints aren't really about the dog; more likely, the barking has become a focal point for other conflicts and ill feelings between neighbors.

When does barking become a problem?

Everyone knows that barking is normal dog behavior. Barking is communication. Expecting a dog to never bark is like asking a person to never talk. Most dog owners want their dogs to bark in certain situations and not in others.

Neighbors who don't own dogs however, might be just as happy if they never had to listen to canines communicating. Yet choosing to live in either an urban or suburban area means people must accept a certain amount of noise pollution. This includes not only barking dogs, but children playing, noisy lawn mowers and weed-whackers, motorcycles, and the occasional loud party.

Whether your dog's barking is a problem is determined not only by your dog's actual behavior, but when and where it occurs, and also who hears it. Even a bout of normal barking can be perceived as nuisance barking if it wakes you up at 2:00 a.m. or occurs at 2:00 p.m. right underneath the window of a neighbor who works from home.

Consequences of canine barking problems

For your community

If your dog's barking is causing a problem, it can create a variety of negative consequences for you, your dog and your community. Responding to a complaint about your barking dog costs your community money and time. Animal control agencies, prosecutors and courts can be tied up dealing with violations of barking dog ordinances and therefore have less time to deal with more serious animal issues.

For you

Your dog's barking can put your relationship with him at risk. If your dog becomes more of an annoyance and less enjoyable to have around, he may not remain in your home.

Even if you would never, ever consider giving up your dog, his noisy behavior may result in sleepless nights, disruptions in your activities, general aggravation, angry neighbors, worry about how your dog is affecting others, and even fines or other legal actions from your community.

For your dog

If your dog is barking excessively, it likely is having a negative effect on his well-being. Fear, boredom, frustration and physical pain–all common causes of barking–are stressors that can compromise your dog's welfare.

And unless your dog's behavior changes, you may be forced to restrict certain areas of your house or yard that your dog can occupy, which may also impact his quality of life. If left outside, your barking dog is at risk of abuse by angry neighbors. External pressures may force you to consider debarking your dog or even giving him up.

All of these negative consequences should provide strong motivation for you to prevent or resolve your dog's barking problem. All dog owners have a responsibility to keep their dogs from becoming nuisances to the community and to meet their dogs' behavioral needs.

Where should you start?

Have you been at a loss for how to decrease your dog's excessive barking? Do you feel you've "tried everything" without success? Chances are you haven't tried the right thing. All the things you've tried before may be irrelevant and ineffective because they didn't address the "why" of your dog's barking. You can't choose the best course of action until you have determined the why.

Finding the solution to the problem is the last step, not the first. The first step is gathering information and recording it in a logical form. The tools to do so are in this book.

Overview of the book

In Chapter Two you'll learn about **My Dog's Barking Profile**, a unique questionnaire that helps you gather the information you need to determine the cause of your dog's barking. Read the rest of the chapters in order, completing **My Dog's Barking Profile** as you go. By doing so, you'll free yourself from wasted time and effort doing things that don't make sense and may be doomed to fail.

Chapters Three and Four help you gather the information you need to fill out the **Barking Profile**. Chapter Three describes the different kinds of sounds that dogs make. Chapter Four helps you analyze how your dog looks when he barks, what he is doing when he is barking, and when, where, and at what he is barking. It also explains how to use **My Dog's Body Posture Checklist**, an important tool for identifying how your dog looks while barking. All of this information is crucial for analyzing your dog's behavior.

In Chapter Five you'll learn how to use **My Dog's Barking Profile** and our unique **BarkCharts** to determine the cause of your dog's barking.

Our unique **Positive Proaction Plan**©, a five-part strategy to prevent, manage and resolve most barking problems, is presented in Chapter Six. You can use this plan for your dog's barking behavior, as well as other behavior issues with your dog. Chapter Seven explains the major reasons dogs vocalize, and the distinguishing features of each type of motivation. It also tells you how to use the **Positive Proaction Plan**© to manage and resolve each of the different kinds of barking problems.

In Chapter Eight you'll learn how different kinds of anti-bark devices work, the pros and cons of each, and how to use them effectively and humanely. Surgical debarking is also discussed. Chapter Nine tells you what to look for if you decide to seek professional help for your dog's barking behavior.

In Chapter Ten you'll find references, resources and useful Web sites to help you resolve your dog's barking problem. At the back of the book you'll also find copies of **My Dog's Barking Profile**, **My Dog's Body Posture Checklist**, **The Key to My Dog's Barking Postures**, and the **BarkCharts**. These are important forms that you will tear out and use as you read the book.

Don't be tempted to skip to the solution chapters first. That takes you back to the faulty approach of seeking a solution before you understand the problem. By taking haphazard, try-this-try-that steps, or relying on supposed "quick fixes" *before* you understand the behavior, you risk making your dog's barking worse and/or creating other problems. This leads us to an important discussion of things NOT to do when dealing with your dog's barking problem.

What <u>Not</u> To Do About Your Dog's Barking

When you are analyzing your dog's barking and weighing the different solution options, it's important to think about what NOT do. Taking the wrong steps to deal with the issue can make things worse for your dog. You can unintentionally intensify your dog's barking, create other problems, and/or have a negative impact on your dog's well-being and quality of life.

Please take this list of "don'ts" seriously. There are no quick fixes for barking, or any other kind of behavior problem. Attempts at such often backfire and in the long-term create more problems.

- Don't take action until you understand why your dog is barking.
- Don't use punishment as the only way to resolve the problem.
- Don't use punishment if you cannot meet the criteria to make it effective (see Chapter Six).
- Never use punishment with pain, illness, fear or separation anxiety problems. It will only make things worse.
- Don't muzzle your dog to prevent barking. This will not change your dog's motivation to bark and may be harmful to your dog's health. It is particularly dangerous to leave your dog unattended while muzzled. It is much too easy for her to catch or even hang herself on something, plus she cannot pant sufficiently and it is difficult, if not impossible, for her to drink water. Your dog may also injure herself trying to get the muzzle off.
- Avoid crating or confining your dog in small areas if her barking is motivated by fears, separation anxiety, boredom or frustration. This is likely to either make the problem worse or create new problem behaviors.

- While training classes are very beneficial for many reasons, and we highly recommend them, "obedience classes" will not directly decrease problem barking. Barking is not an obedience problem. If your dog is barking excessively because she's lonely and bored, spending more time with her in any way, including enrolling her in a training class, is a good thing.

- "Dominance exercises" such as rolling your dog, scruff shaking her, or pinning her on her back, do not improve barking problems and may create fear or aggression problems. Barking is not a dominance problem.

With these things in mind, it's time to introduce you to **My Dog's Barking Profile** so you can get started analyzing your dog's behavior.

"A dog can express more with his tail in minutes than his owner can express with his tongue in hours."

— Anonymous

Chapter Two
My Dog's Barking Profile©: What You Must Know About Your Dog's Behavior Before You Do Anything

Your dog's excessive barking is not an obedience problem, nor is it a dominance problem. These kinds of explanations are not only inaccurate, but much too vague to be of any help. Dogs bark and make other noises for more reasons than they can shake their sticks at! Until now, you've been guessing at why your dog is being so noisy, and likely haven't had a thorough understanding of barking behavior. To take the guesswork out of the process and avoid overlooking factors that are influencing your dog's behavior, you need to obtain several pieces of information:

- the actual sounds your dog makes
- how he looks when he's barking
- where he's barking
- when he's barking
- what he's barking at (if anything)
- what other behaviors he's doing when he's barking

By filling out **My Dog's Barking Profile**, there are samples at the end of the book, you have a systematic way of identifying and recording this information.

Don't expect to be able to answer all the questions right now. Even if you think you can complete the **Profile** now, as you read the next two chapters, you'll find you need to gather more information to fully answer each question.

Then, once you've completed the **Profile**, you'll use it in Chapter Five to determine the reason for your dog's barking so you will then be able to choose the best course of action.

You'll find copies of **My Dog's Barking Profile** at the back of this book. Tear out one copy now and begin filling it out as you read the next chapters. Fill out the **Profile** in pencil so you can make changes if necessary. You have an extra copy in the back of the book if you need to start over. If you have more than one dog that has a barking problem, make an extra copy of **My Dog's Barking Profile** for each of them.

Completing **My Dog's Barking Profile**

Creating a **Profile** for your dog is crucial because different types of problems require different solutions. Don't forget that your dog may be barking for more than one reason and therefore may require more than one type of solution.

Don't waste time, money or effort in trying things that are unlikely to work because they don't go to the "why" of the behavior. Be smarter than your dog. Take the time to understand his behavior before rushing to try things that will be useless from the start.

Question 1 asks you to describe the sounds your dog is making. Although we talk about "barking" problems, it's very possible that your dog is actually doing something other than barking. Chapter Three describes a variety of sounds that dogs make, and under what conditions you are likely to hear different types of vocalizations.

Question 2 asks you to describe what your dog looks like when he's vocalizing. This is critical information. If your dog is growling, it has a very different meaning if he's in a play-bow versus in an offensively threatening posture. You'll learn about body postures and how to "read" your dog in Chapter Four.

Chapter Four not only describes six body features to look at, but how to interpret and categorize what you see. You'll complete a **Checklist** from your observations that you will use to answer Question 2 in the **Profile**.

Questions 3-8 ask about the what, when and where of your dog's barking behavior. The pattern of the barking helps you to distinguish between motivations. If your dog's barking is motivated by separation anxiety for example, the what, when and where answers will be very different than if he's alarm or alerting barking. Questions 10 and 11 also help you identify a separation anxiety problem.

The answer to Question 9 will give you a clue as to whether your dog's barking is a type of compulsive behavior.

If you can't supply all of the information asked for in **My Dog's Barking Profile**, you will need to do some detective work. You may need to audiotape or videotape your dog to get the information you require. You may need to park down the block and listen, or acquire more information from your animal control officer about what he or she has seen or heard from your dog.

The complaining neighbor's description of your dog's behavior may not be reliable. If you try to gain additional information from cooperative neighbors, ask them questions similar to those in **My Dog's Barking Profile**. It's a good idea to interview more than one neighbor to avoid biases, and because different neighbors may observe your dog at different times.

My Dog's Barking Profile

Try to answer all the questions in this **Profile**. The more information you have, the more successful you will be at identifying why your dog is barking and finding the right solution. Your dog's barking problem may have more than one cause. Check all the boxes that apply.

1. What is your dog doing? ❑ Barking ❑ Howling
❑ Whining/whimpering ❑ Yelping ❑ Growling ❑ Screaming

   What kind of emotion do you think your dog has when he barks?
Does he sound: ❑ Happy ❑ Excited ❑ Threatening ❑ Fearful
❑ In pain ❑ Don't know

2. What does your dog look like when he is barking?
❑ Looks or acts friendly ❑ Looks or acts offensively threatening
❑ Looks or acts defensively threatening ❑ Looks or acts fearful
❑ Looks or acts playful ❑ Looks or acts alert ❑ Paces, circles, limps, hides, looks ill or in pain ❑ Don't know

3. Where is your dog barking? ❑ Inside house ❑ In a fenced yard
❑ In an unfenced area of property ❑ When tied on rope/chain
❑ When running free or at large ❑ When in a vehicle ❑ When on leash walks ❑ When he is prevented from getting to other dogs, people or things ❑ When isolated from other people or dogs or when he is in a barren environment ❑ When he is at other locations
Explain : _____

4. When does the barking occur?
Days of the week _____
Time of day _____
❑ When someone is home ❑ When no one is home
❑ Only when left alone or when he is separated from people.

   If it occurs when no one is home, does it begin within a half hour after your dog is separated from people? ❑ Yes ❑ No

   If it occurs at certain times or on certain days of the week, are there specific things happening at those times that may cause the barking (such as the mail delivery person arriving)? ❑ Yes ❑ No
If yes, what is happening? _____

My Dog's Barking Profile – continued

5. How consistent is the barking in this (these) location(s) and time(s)?
   ❏ Almost every time ❏ Better than half the time
   ❏ Less than half the time ❏ Very erratic, occurs rarely

   Is there a consistent pattern to the barking? ❏ Yes ❏ No

6. Is your dog barking at something? ❏ Yes ❏ No, appears to bark at nothing. If yes, go to question 7, if no, skip to question 9.

7. What is your dog barking at? ❏ Your family members ❏ Other people ❏ Other dogs ❏ Other animals (cats, squirrels, birds, etc.)

8. What is your dog barking at? ❏ Inanimate moving objects (vehicles, hot air balloons, thunderstorms, the wind) ❏ Inanimate stationary objects (house, parked cars, trees, rocks, etc.) ❏ Other
   Explain:_____

9. When your dog barks, does he seem oblivious to everything around him and difficult to interrupt? ❏ Yes ❏ No

10. What else does your dog do when he is barking? ❏ Scratches or digs at doors, windows, gates or fences ❏ Chews or bites at doors, windows, gates or fences ❏ Urinates or defecates ❏ Destroys other things (clothes, furniture, etc.) ❏ Other behavior
    Explain:_____

11. How does your dog act when you leave and return?
    Does he act agitated, anxious, fearful or depressed when people get ready to leave home? ❏ Yes ❏ No

    Is he overly excited when you return home? ❏ Yes ❏ No

    Does he follow you around excessively when you are home?
    ❏ Yes ❏ No

12. Other relevant information and notes:

    _____

    _____

    _____

    _____

"When a dog wags her tail and barks at the same time, how do you know which end to believe?"

– Anonymous

Chapter Three
The Sounds Dogs Make

(Use this information to answer Question 1 on **My Dog's Barking Profile**.)

Although you may describe your dog as having a "barking problem," you know your dog makes a variety of sounds, each of which has a different motivation and message. Your neighbor may tell you your dog is "barking," but she may actually be whining, howling and/or whimpering. To keep things simple, throughout this book we will refer to problem vocalizations as "barking," unless we are referring to a specific vocalization that isn't barking, like howling or growling.

You're probably already good at interpreting what your dog is trying to tell you by how she sounds. Your dog sounds different if she's barking when she's frightened or when the doorbell rings, or when she's trying to entice you to play. As the first step in determining the "why" of your dog's behavior, you need to identify all the sounds she's making.

It may even be helpful for you to record the sounds your dog makes if she's vocalizing only when you're away. Use a voice-activated recorder, or ask a cooperative neighbor for help. If you find your "barking" dog is actually whining, howling, and/or yelping, this will provide the first insight into why she's being so noisy.

Barking

This short, discrete sound is familiar to everyone. Barking seems to be one of the defining characteristics of domestic dogs. Wolves and other wild canids (coyotes, foxes) bark very little, while dogs bark frequently and in many different situations. It's likely that through domestication we've created dogs that bark readily and frequently in comparison to their wild relatives.

In subsequent sections of this book, you'll learn about the many different motivations for barking. Dogs may bark in greeting, in play, as a call for attention, as a call to attract others or to alert others, as a threat, when afraid or frustrated, or as a response to pain. Dogs bark both when they are alone or in a group.

Howling

This high-pitched vocalization is significantly longer in duration than the discrete bark. Howling can occur as a greeting, a request for contact with others, or as a group vocalization. A popular belief is that northern breeds such as huskies and malamutes howl more than other breeds, but this has not been systemati-cally studied. Dalmatians, basset hounds and beagles are also known for howl-ing. Like barking, howling can be socially facilitated; that is, sounds that one dog makes can recruit others into vocalizing as well.

Growling

Growling is a low-pitched vocalization that can be short or long. Dogs often use it as a threat or warning, but also when they are afraid, playing or, rarely, in greet-ings. You can probably tell the difference when your dog is growling menacingly or just playing.

Yelping

Experts in canine behavior state that yelping is common in dogs, but rare in other canids. Dogs yelp when they are afraid, in distress or in pain. Less commonly, they may also yelp when playing, during greetings, to seek attention or contact, or when frustrated. Yelping is also more common in puppies than adult dogs. Young puppies may also produce other sounds that have been called grunts and mews.

Whimper/whine

Longer duration yelps become whines or whimpers, and one can blend into the other. Dogs use these sounds in many of the same contexts as yelps. Puppies often yelp, whine or whimper when separated from Mom or littermates, when hungry, cold, or otherwise uncomfortable.

Screaming

This is a loud, high-pitched vocalization that is unmistakable. Dogs most often scream when they are in pain or are fearful or distressed, but this sound may also be part of a submissive display during a social conflict.

Two other sounds that dogs make are panting and tooth snapping. Panting is a low-pitched sound made when dogs are hot, exercising, playing, excited, fearful, or distressed. Tooth snapping is a low-intensity sound made by closing the jaws together quickly. It can occur when a dog is playing, threatening, in conflict or distressed. Neither one by itself usually causes serious problems so we won't talk about them further.

When you listen to your dog, or a recording of her sounds, you may discover that she's using more than one type of sound to make the noise your neighbors are complaining about. For example, a dog that's distressed at being left alone (separation anxiety) may bark and then "slide" into a yelp or whine. A threatening dog may mix barks with growls.

Enter the information about the sounds your dog makes in Question 1 of your **Barking Profile**. Enter all of the sounds your dog is making when she is a problem. Sometimes you can identify the emotion in your dog's sounds. For many people, an aggressive bark sounds different from a happy, playful bark. If you think you can identify an emotion, such as threat, fear or happiness in your dog's barking, mark this down in Question 1 as well. This part of the question may be easier to answer after you've read Chapter Four.

"A barking dog is often more useful than a sleeping lion."

– Washington Irving

Chapter Four
The Body Language and Behaviors of Dogs

(Use this information to answer Questions 2-12 on **My Dog's Barking Profile**.)

Barking and other vocalizations are only one type of communication. Dogs also use body postures and facial expressions to communicate their intentions and emotional states. By first observing, then interpreting both what you see and hear, you can make better predictions about what your dog is doing, or is likely to do, and why.

You need to know what your dog looks like when he's vocalizing. If you just listen to an audiotape of the sounds your dog is making, you may not be able to tell whether he's threatening or fearful. Find out, either by observing your dog yourself, videotaping him, or asking your neighbors what your dog looks like when vocalizing.

There is no single feature of your dog's body language that you can rely on to understand his behavior. It's a myth, for example, that a dog wagging his tail won't bite.

Each feature may communicate similar or distinctly different motivations. Your dog's ears may be back, indicating fear, while his tail might be held high, which indicates offensiveness or arousal. When features don't agree with one another, your dog may be confused, conflicted or unsure about how to behave.

Below you'll find a sample of **My Dog's Body Posture Checklist**. This **Checklist** makes it easy to record your observations of your dog's behavior while he is barking. The **Checklist** can then be used to interpret his behavior. Copies of the **Checklist** are in the back of the book. Tear one out now and fill it out while you are watching your dog bark, or from the descriptions of others.

Complete **My Dog's Body Posture Checklist** for all of the six features listed (overall body carriage, ear carriage, tail carriage, eyes and gaze, facial expression, hackles up [called piloerection]). Check all the characteristics that apply. Observe and record what you see before you interpret your observations. You are likely to miss an important feature if you try jumping to interpretations without careful observations.

In the back of the book you will find copies of **The Key to My Dog's Body Postures**. Tear one out now. After you've completed the **Checklist**, transfer your observations for each body feature into each of the behavioral categories in the

Key to My Dog's Body Postures. For example if you observed your dog's hackles up, you would put a check mark in the box next to number 10 under Offensive threats and number 10 under Defensive threats. Continue down the **Checklist**, recording all the postures you saw in the appropriate categories of the **Key**. The drawings in Figures 1 through 6 show you what these different body postures look like, and will help you to correctly identify your dog's motivations. If your dog's postures don't fit neatly into one category, it's because there is more than one reason behind the behavior. Just copy your observations into all the possible categories that fit the observations.

To help you understand how **My Dog's Body Posture Checklist** and the **Key to My Dog's Body Postures** work together, review the following samples for a fictitious dog named Fido. Follow along to see how the observations led to the conclusion that Fido was fearful when he was barking.

If you purchased our Canine Body Postures™ videotape with this book, stop now and watch the tape. The video will be very helpful to you in interpreting your dog's postures. If you don't have the tape, see the order form and resource list at the back of this book.

My Dog's Body Posture Checklist – Sample for Fido

Record your observations. Put a check mark next to the elements you observe when your dog is barking.

My dog's overall body carriage

- ☐ Stiff legs, upright stance
- ☐ Upright stance, not stiff
- ☑ Crouched
- ☐ Body weight shifted to forequarters
- ☐ Body weight shifted to hindquarters
- ☐ Sitting or lying down
- ☐ Directly facing what he's barking at
- ☐ Turned away or hiding from what he's barking at
- ☑ Moves toward what he's barking at
- ☐ Moves away from what he's barking at
- ☐ Play bows

My dog's ear carriage

- ☐ Ears pricked forward or upright
- ☑ Ears pulled back against head or bent down to the side
- ☐ Variable, may be upright or slightly back
- ☐ Cropped ears

My dog's tail carriage

- ☐ Tail straight up or high
- ☐ Tail carried low, straight out and/or pointing downward
- ☑ Tail tucked between legs
- ☐ Tail stationary, not moving
- ☐ Tail wagging furiously and rapidly from side to side
- ☐ Tail wagging slowly and deliberately from side to side
- ☐ Variable, may be slightly lowered or held high
- ☐ Docked or no tail

My Dog's Body Posture Checklist – Sample for Fido

My dog's eyes and gaze

- ❑ Dog staring directly at what he's barking at
- ☑ Dog looks away from a direct stare, avoids eye contact
- ❑ Eyes open normally, soft without a hard stare
- ☑ Eyes wide open, whites of eyes exaggerated
- ❑ Pupils (center black part of eye) dilated

My dog's facial expression

- ❑ Mouth closed and relaxed
- ❑ Mouth open but relaxed
- ❑ Baring teeth by retracting lips vertically (up and down) from the front of the mouth, canine teeth mostly visible
- ❑ Baring teeth by retracting lips horizontally from the corners or back of the mouth, molars or side teeth visible
- ❑ Snaps or tries to bite
- ❑ Teeth not showing but muzzle tense and/or puckered
- ❑ Submissive grin

Are My dog's hackles up? (Piloerection or erect hair)

- ❑ Yes
- ☑ No
- ❑ Partly

Key to My Dog's Body Postures – Sample for Fido

(Use this information to answer Question 2 on **My Dog's Barking Profile**.)

Interpret your observations. Put a check mark in the box next to the characteristic you checked on the **Checklist**. Go through all the descriptions below and check the appropriate boxes.

Offensive threats (Figure 1)

Dogs threaten to warn others to go away or stop what they are doing. Threatening dogs may or may not escalate to biting. Dogs who are offensively threatening are not afraid. They are demonstrating their willingness to initiate conflict or fight, and may move or lunge toward their opponent. The body postures associated with offensive threats make the dog appear larger and more intimidating. Offensively threatening dogs can show one or more of the following:

Figure 1. Offensively threatening

© Courtesy ASPCA.

❑   1.   Stands tall with a stiff body posture

❑   2.   Body weight may be shifted to the forequarters so the dog is ready to lunge forward

❑   3.   May lunge, snap at, or chase others

❑   4.   Tail straight up, it may be wagging slowly and deliberately

❑   5.   Ears up and forward

❑   6.   Direct eye contact or staring

❑   7.   Teeth bared from the front of the mouth (vertical retraction of lips)

❑   8.   Teeth may not be showing but muzzle may be tense or puckered

❑   9.   Snaps or tries to bite

❑ 10.   Hackles up

Defensive threats (Figure 2)

The defensive dog is both threatening and afraid. While such dogs are still warning others to stay away, they aren't interested in initiating a conflict. If left alone, they usually won't bite or attack. The body postures associated with defensive threats serve to make the dog appear smaller and less of a target. Defensively threatening dogs will show one or more fearful postures (1-6) **and** one or more threatening postures (7-10):

Figure 2. Defensively threatening

© Courtesy ASPCA.

☑ 1. Crouched or lowered body posture

❑ 2. Dog may shift body weight more to the rear quarters, as though leaning away from the opponent

☑ 3. May move away from opponent

☑ 4. Ears laid back or down

☑ 5. Tail straight out, down, or even tucked between the legs, not wagging

☑ 6. Dog usually looks away from a direct stare

❑ 7. Teeth bared from the back of the mouth (horizontal retraction of lips)

❑ 8. Teeth may not be showing but muzzle may be tense and/or puckered

❑ 9. Snaps or tries to bite

❑ 10. Hackles may be up

Fearful or submissive behavior (Figures 3 and 4)

Dogs can be fearful without being threatening. Submissive and fearful behaviors overlap each other. Dogs show submission only during social interactions, but can show fearful behaviors toward sounds and objects as well. Fearful or submissive dogs can show one or more of the following:

Figure 3. Submissive or fearful

© Courtesy ASPCA.

☑ 1. Crouched body posture or lying down, even rolled over on the back exposing the belly

☐ 2. May run away or try to avoid the other person, or the fearful event or stimulus

☑ 3. Ears laid back or down

☑ 4. Tail down or tucked between the legs

☑ 5. Looks away and avoids direct eye contact

☑ 6. Eyes wide open, whites of eyes exaggerated

☐ 7. May retract the lips into a submissive grin

☐ 8. Mouth may be open but relaxed

Figure 4. Submissive

© Courtesy ASPCA.

Alert or orienting behavior (Figure 5)

When something catches your dog's attention, his body posture changes from being relaxed to being focused or directed to something specific. He's not yet decided whether to be friendly, fearful or threatening–he's just paying attention. Dogs who are alerting can display one or more of the following:

Figure 5. Alert or orienting

© Courtesy ASPCA.

☐ 1. Upright body posture, but usually not as stiff as the offensive dog–he may even be lying down

☐ 2. Body and gaze directed at the "thing" that has captured his attention

☐ 3. Ears upright

☐ 4. Tail variable, may be down or held high

☐ 5. Eyes open normally without a hard stare

☐ 6. Mouth open and relaxed, or closed and relaxed

Friendly behavior

Surprisingly, friendly behavior is a little difficult to describe. Friendly dogs indicate a willingness to interact and they solicit attention. They may show elements of submission and play as well. Friendly dogs can show one or more of the following:

- ❏ 1. Body posture relaxed, not stiff-legged, may be slightly crouched or lowered
- ❏ 2. Moves towards the person or other dog
- ❏ 3. Variable ear carriage–may be upright or slightly back
- ❏ 4. Variable tail carriage–may be slightly lowered or held high, usually not tucked
- ❏ 5. If the tail is wagging, it should be a relaxed, yet rapid wag, not slow and deliberate
- ❏ 6. Eyes will appear "soft," without a hard stare
- ❏ 7. Mouth may be open or closed but is relaxed
- ❏ 8. May show other elements of submissive behavior
- ❏ 9. May lick, nudge or sniff people's hands or arms

Playful behavior (Figure 6)

Playful, friendly and submissive behaviors often have elements in common. Dogs may show friendly behaviors in conjunction with or preceding playful behavior. Playful dogs can show one or more of the following:

Figure 6. Playful

- ❏ 1. A play bow
- ❏ 2. May paw at play partner
- ❏ 3. Variable ear carriage–may be upright or slightly back
- ❏ 4. Variable tail carriage–may be slightly lowered or held high, usually not tucked
- ❏ 5. Other friendly behaviors that alternate with threats and submissive behavior

Once you have filled out the **Key to My Dog's Body Postures**, transfer this information to Question 2 of **My Dog's Barking Profile**. In general, the behavioral category with the most check marks is the one that best describes your dog's behavior when barking. If your dog appears to have several motivations at the same time, that is, you have more than one category with more than one check mark, enter all the interpretations that apply.

You'll notice that for our Sample for Fido, his behavior fit five of the ten characteristics for defensive threats and five of the eight characteristics of fearful or submissive behavior. His behavior most closely fits with fearful or submissive behavior. It doesn't fit defensive threatening behavior because all of the elements checked in this category were fearful (1-6), there were no threat elements (7-10) such as showing of teeth, snapping or biting.

Behaviors Associated with Barking

(Use this information to answer Questions 3-12 on **My Dog's Barking Profile**.)

Now you have two pieces of information–what sounds your dog is making and what he looks like when he's making them. You need several more pieces of information before you can reasonably decide why your dog is barking.

First, you need to know the pattern of your dog's barking–when, where, at what, and how often he's barking or vocalizing. Try to answer Questions 3 through 8 in **My Dog's Barking Profile**. If you can't answer these questions, try to gather more information.

Second, you need to know what else he might be doing while he's vocalizing. Is your dog running in circles, or running up and down the fence? Is he pawing or jumping at the door or window? Is he just sitting in the middle of the living room or the yard howling? The behaviors associated with your dog's barking provide important clues about his motivations.

If you've already observed your dog barking, obtained descriptions of your dog's behavior from others, or videotaped your dog, you should now have all of this information. Use what you know to answer Questions 9 and 10 in the **Profile**.

Question 11 has to do with how your dog responds when you are with him, when you leave or return. Your dog may not be barking at these times, but the answers to these questions can be important in identifying a separation anxiety problem. Mark all the answers that apply.

Finally, Question 12 asks you to list all the other relevant information you may have that isn't covered elsewhere. Here you might note that the problem started right after a particularly bad thunderstorm, or that your dog only barks at one particular neighbor. This information may help you figure out what is causing the problem or how best to solve it.

By knowing a) the sounds your dog makes, b) his body postures, c) when, where, at what and how often he's vocalizing, and d) what else he's doing when he's barking, you'll be able to fill out the **BarkCharts** in Chapter Five.

Chapter Five
Determining the Cause of Your Dog's Barking

If you've completed your dog's **Barking Profile**, you are now ready to determine the cause of your dog's barking. The goal of the **BarkCharts** is to help you decide what is motivating your dog's behavior so you can learn what will and will not help the problem.

You will use your answers from the **Barking Profile** to work through the **BarkCharts** found at the back of the book. Tear them out now. The **BarkCharts** are designed to identify the major categories of problem barking. They are the best "self-help" assessment tools you can find.

These flow charts will lead you to one or more of the categories found in the ovals of the **BarkCharts** and discussed in following chapters. The categories are also listed in Box 1.

Start with **BarkChart** 1 and follow the arrows. You will see boxes, diamonds, ovals and arrows. The boxes ask about the information you included in **My Dog's Barking Profile**. The bold "Q" followed by a number in each information box refers to the specific question in the **Profile**. Use your answers to these questions to respond to the statements in each information box.

The diamonds are points where you need to make decisions. Your "yes" or "no" responses in the diamonds will lead you through the flow chart.

The arrows direct you to the next point in the flow chart depending on your answer. The ovals are end points with the categories of barking.

What if the answer to a question on **My Dog's Barking Profile** leads you to respond with both "yes" and "no" to an information box? For example, suppose in Question 6 your dog barks at something sometimes and seems to bark at nothing other times. Work through the **BarkCharts** with the "yes" answer, then go back and work through it with the "no" answer. You'll find that your dog's barking may have multiple causes, which is common in some situations. In this case, several different solution plans may be needed to resolve all the problems.

There are also some ovals that say "Get More Information." This means that you can't identify the possible causes of the barking from what you know now, so follow the suggestions given previously (on page 16) about how to obtain more information.

To help you understand how **My Dog's Barking Profile** and the **BarkCharts** work together, review the sample of **My Dog's Barking Profile** and the **BarkCharts** that follow, for a fictitious dog named Fido. Be sure you follow along and can see how the information led to the conclusion that Fido was barking because he was afraid of the garbage truck.

In Chapter Seven we'll describe the categories of barking problems listed in each of the endpoint ovals. If the **BarkCharts** have accurately categorized your dog's behavior, you should recognize the description of your dog's behavior in these categories. Chapters Six and Seven will help you decide how to get your dog to bark less.

If for any reason you can't work through the **BarkCharts**, this is an indication you need to work with a behavior professional to identify the causes of the barking and to develop a plan for resolution. Or you may prefer working one-on-one with someone, in person, who is experienced with barking problems. A behavior consultant can create a custom-designed behavior modification plan based on a personal behavioral interview and observations of your dog.

Refer to Chapter Nine on selecting trainers and behavior consultants, or visit **www.AnimalBehaviorAssociates.com** or **www.BarkingHelp.com** to schedule a consultation with us.

THE TYPES OF PROBLEM VOCALIZATIONS IN DOGS

- Aggressive vocalizations
- Alerting or greeting vocalizations
- Playful vocalizations
- Attention-seeking vocalizations
- Comfort-seeking and boredom vocalizations
- Fear/distress/anxiety vocalizations
- Separation anxiety vocalizations
- Painful or medically caused vocalizations
- Frustration vocalizations
- Compulsive vocalizations

Box 1

My Dog's Barking Profile – Sample for Fido

Try to answer all the questions in this **Profile**. The more information you have, the more successful you will be at identifying why your dog is barking and finding the right solution. Your dog's barking problem may have more than one cause. Check all the boxes that apply.

1. What is your dog doing? ☑ Barking ❑ Howling
    ☑ Whining/whimpering ❑ Yelping ❑ Growling ❑ Screaming

    What kind of emotion do you think your dog has when he barks?
    Does he sound: ❑ Happy ❑ Excited ❑ Threatening ❑ Fearful
    ❑ In pain ☑ Don't know

2. What does your dog look like when he is barking?
    ❑ Looks or acts friendly ❑ Looks or acts offensively threatening
    ❑ Looks or acts defensively threatening ☑ Looks or acts fearful
    ❑ Looks or acts playful ❑ Looks or acts alert ❑ Paces, circles, limps,
    hides, looks ill or in pain ❑ Don't know

3. Where is your dog barking? ❑ Inside house ☑ In a fenced yard
    ❑ In unfenced area of property ❑ When tied on rope/chain
    ❑ When running free or at large ❑ When in a vehicle ❑ When on leash
    walks ❑ When he is prevented from getting to other dogs, people or
    things ❑ When isolated from other people or dogs or when he is in a
    barren environment ❑ When he is at other locations
    Explain : _____

4. When does the barking occur?
    Days of the week _____Tuesday_____
    Time of day _____mornings_____
    ❑ When someone is home ☑ When no one is home
    ❑ Only when left alone or when he is separated from people

    If it occurs when no one is home, does it begin within a half hour after
    your dog is separated from people? ❑ Yes ☑ No

    If it occurs at certain times or days of the week, are there specific things
    happening at those times that may cause the barking (such as the mail
    delivery person arriving)? ☑ Yes ❑ No
    If yes, what is going on? _____garbage pickup_____

My Dog's Barking Profile – Sample for Fido – continued

5. How consistent is the barking in this (these) location(s) and time(s)?
    ☑ Almost every time ☐ Better than half the time
    ☐ Less than half the time ☐ Very erratic, occurs rarely

    Is there a consistent pattern to the barking? ☑ Yes ☐ No

6. Is your dog barking at something? ☑ Yes ☐ No, appears to bark at nothing. If yes, go to Question 7. If no, skip to Question 9.

7. What is your dog barking at? ☐ Your family members ☐ Other people ☐ Other dogs ☐ Other animals (cats, squirrels, birds, etc.)

8. What is your dog barking at? ☑ Inanimate moving objects (vehicles, hot air balloons, thunderstorms, the wind) ☐ Inanimate stationary objects (house, parked cars, trees, rocks, etc.) ☐ Other

    Explain: _He barks at the garbage truck_

9. When your dog barks, does he seem oblivious to everything around him and hard to stop? ☐ Yes ☑ No

10. What else does your dog do when he is barking? ☐ Scratches or digs at doors, windows, gates or fences ☐ Chews or bites at doors, windows, gates or fences ☐ Urinates or defecates ☐ Destroys other things (clothes, furniture, etc.) ☐ Other behavior
    Explain:_____

11. How does your dog look and act when you leave and return? Does he act agitated, anxious, fearful or depressed when people get ready to leave home? ☐ Yes ☑ No

    Is he overly excited when you return home? ☑ Yes ☐ No

    Does he follow you around excessively when you are home?
    ☐ Yes ☑ No

12. Other relevant information and notes:

    _____

    _____

    _____

    _____

BarkCharts

Chart 1 - SAMPLE FOR FIDO

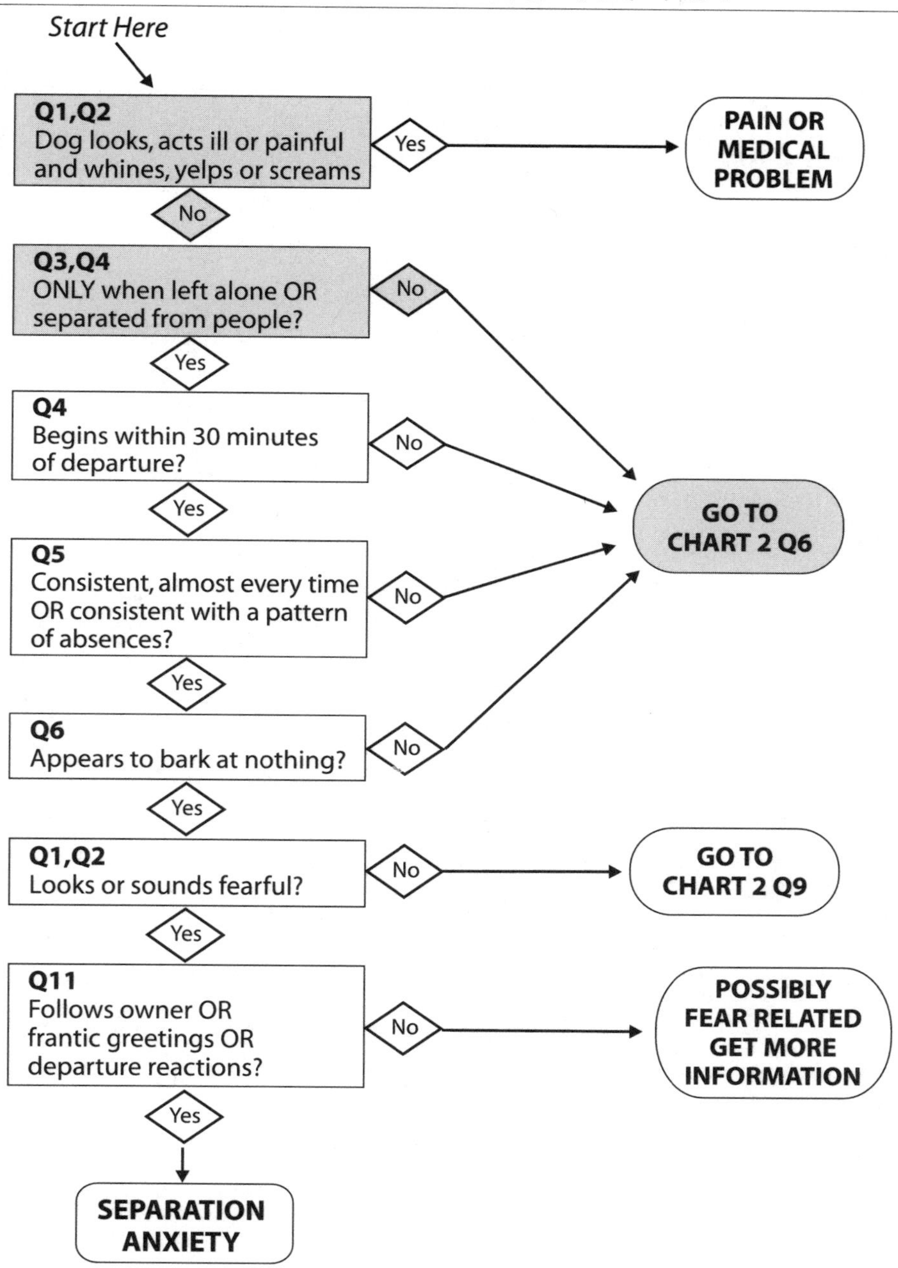

Start Here

Q1,Q2
Dog looks, acts ill or painful and whines, yelps or screams — Yes → **PAIN OR MEDICAL PROBLEM**

No ↓

Q3,Q4
ONLY when left alone OR separated from people? — No → **GO TO CHART 2 Q6**

Yes ↓

Q4
Begins within 30 minutes of departure? — No → **GO TO CHART 2 Q6**

Yes ↓

Q5
Consistent, almost every time OR consistent with a pattern of absences? — No → **GO TO CHART 2 Q6**

Yes ↓

Q6
Appears to bark at nothing? — No → **GO TO CHART 2 Q6**

Yes ↓

Q1,Q2
Looks or sounds fearful? — No → **GO TO CHART 2 Q9**

Yes ↓

Q11
Follows owner OR frantic greetings OR departure reactions? — No → **POSSIBLY FEAR RELATED GET MORE INFORMATION**

Yes ↓

SEPARATION ANXIETY

BarkCharts

Chart 2 - SAMPLE FOR FIDO

Complete Chart 1 first

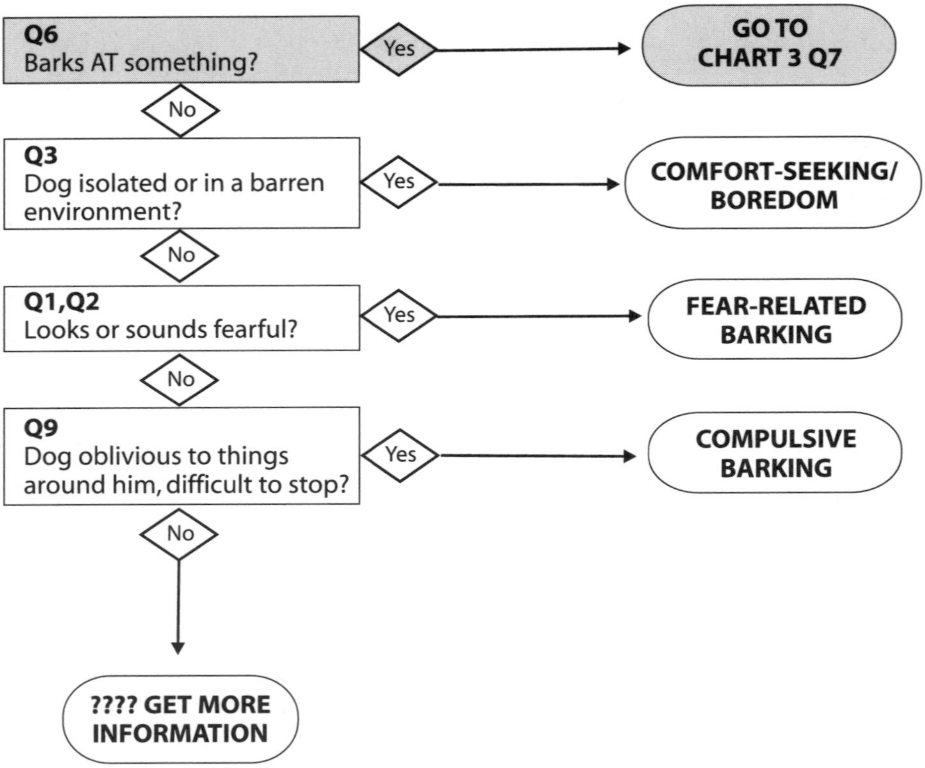

Q6
Barks AT something? —Yes→ **GO TO CHART 3 Q7**

No

Q3
Dog isolated or in a barren environment? —Yes→ **COMFORT-SEEKING/ BOREDOM**

No

Q1,Q2
Looks or sounds fearful? —Yes→ **FEAR-RELATED BARKING**

No

Q9
Dog oblivious to things around him, difficult to stop? —Yes→ **COMPULSIVE BARKING**

No

???? GET MORE INFORMATION

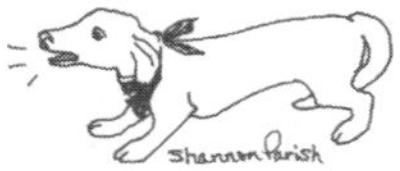

BarkCharts

Chart 3 - SAMPLE FOR FIDO

Complete Chart 1 first

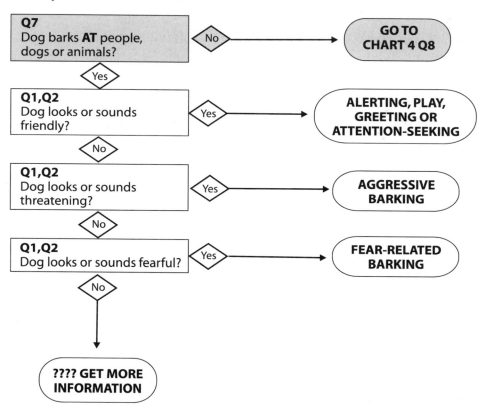

Q7
Dog barks **AT** people, dogs or animals? — No → **GO TO CHART 4 Q8**

Yes ↓

Q1,Q2
Dog looks or sounds friendly? — Yes → **ALERTING, PLAY, GREETING OR ATTENTION-SEEKING**

No ↓

Q1,Q2
Dog looks or sounds threatening? — Yes → **AGGRESSIVE BARKING**

No ↓

Q1,Q2
Dog looks or sounds fearful? — Yes → **FEAR-RELATED BARKING**

No ↓

???? GET MORE INFORMATION

BarkCharts

Chart 4 - SAMPLE FOR FIDO

Complete Chart 1 first

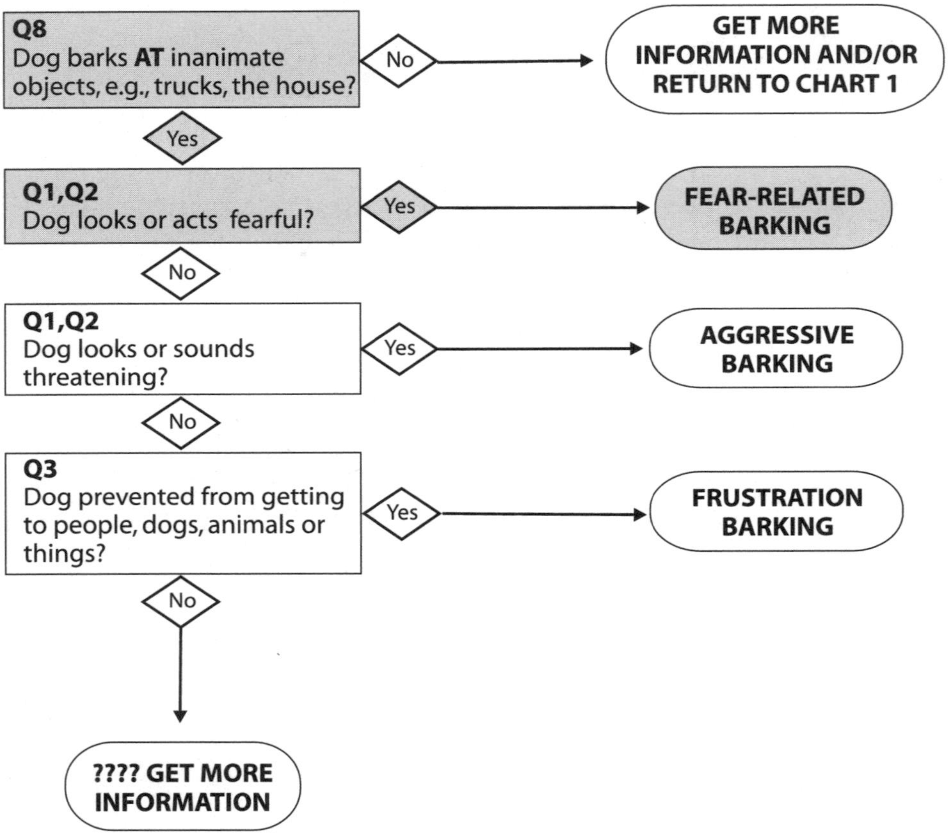

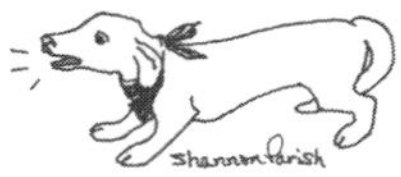

Q8
Dog barks **AT** inanimate objects, e.g., trucks, the house? — No → **GET MORE INFORMATION AND/OR RETURN TO CHART 1**

↓ Yes

Q1,Q2
Dog looks or acts fearful? — Yes → **FEAR-RELATED BARKING**

↓ No

Q1,Q2
Dog looks or sounds threatening? — Yes → **AGGRESSIVE BARKING**

↓ No

Q3
Dog prevented from getting to people, dogs, animals or things? — Yes → **FRUSTRATION BARKING**

↓ No

???? GET MORE INFORMATION

Chapter Six
A Strategy for Dealing with Any Barking Problem:
The Five Step Positive Proaction Plan©

If you've been a pet parent for any length of time, you know it's not always easy to change your dog's behavior. You may feel confused and overwhelmed from conflicting advice or information about what to do.

While there are no simple solutions or quick fixes for pet behavior problems, we have developed a **Five Step Positive Proaction Plan**© to give you a structure to work from. The five steps of the **Plan** are listed in Box 2. The **Plan** is part of our Pet Behavior Wellness Program, and is the basis for preventing and resolving not only barking, but many other behavior problems.

In this chapter we'll explain the steps of the **Positive Proaction Plan**© and give you examples of how you can use each step to modify a barking problem. The importance of each step to your particular problem will vary depending on why your dog is barking. Some steps will be more useful to some types of problems than others. In the next chapter we'll show you how to use the **Plan** to address each of the different categories of barking. You'll find the category or categories of problems that you identified from the **BarkCharts** and specific steps that you can take to address the problem.

If you have difficulty deciding how a step could be used to help your dog, or if your dog's barking is due to multiple causes, you may need a behavior consultant to help you develop the best plan for you and your dog. Refer to Chapter Nine for choosing a trainer or behavior consultant.

If you know or suspect that the barking may be due to pain or medical causes, aggression, fear or separation anxiety, we strongly encourage you to seek professional help from a veterinarian and/or qualified behavior consultant to address the problem. If you don't have a behavior consultant in your area, visit our Web site at **www.BarkingHelp.com** or **www.AnimalBehaviorAssociates.com** and consider a telephone or email consultation with us.

THE FIVE STEPS OF THE POSITIVE PROACTION PLAN

- Catch–and help–your dog do the right thing
- Don't let bad habits develop
- Meet your dog's behavioral needs
- Use the "Take-Away" Method for discouraging unwanted behavior
- Minimize "discipline" (positive punishment) and use it correctly when necessary

Box 2

The Positive Proaction Plan©

1. Catch–and help–your dog do the right thing

Consistently reward your dog for not barking in situations where barking has been, or is likely to be, a problem. If your dog quietly sits at the door to be let in or out, oblige him. If you catch your dog lying quietly in the backyard while neighbors are having a barbecue, reward him with a special chewie. Even better, be proactive and give your dog his special chewie as soon as the neighbors begin their activities. This gives your dog something else to do rather than bark, and also helps your dog feel good about your neighbors' activities.

To learn quiet behavior, your dog will need you to be more proactive in these ways. If your dog begins to bark when he sees someone walking past your house, call your dog to you and reward him for sitting quietly. You are replacing undesired, excited barking behavior with acceptable, quiet behavior.

If your dog is vocalizing due to separation anxiety, you'll have to help him develop the coping skills he needs to tolerate being left alone. You'll likely need professional help from a qualified behaviorist to do this successfully.

How you actually catch and help your dog be quiet will differ depending on why he's vocalizing and the details of your specific situation. The ideas above represent just a few examples of how catching and helping your dog act appropriately–in this case, be quiet–can be implemented.

2. Don't let bad habits develop

The more your dog repeats his excessive, reactive barking, the more it becomes a habit and the more difficult it will be to change. For this reason you must manage your dog's environment to prevent or minimize his contact with his barking triggers. The elements of your dog's world you must manage will depend on why he's barking or vocalizing.

If your dog is showing territorial barking when outside, you can't allow him prolonged, unsupervised time in the yard where he can bark as much as he wants all day long. Letting your dog think it's his job to "protect" the house is a recipe for problems. You may need to leave your dog inside and have someone give him a "potty break" during the day.

If you encourage or passively allow "on patrol" alerting behavior at every little thing he sees or hears, you are allowing a bad habit to develop. Teach your dog to sit quietly in return for a food treat rather than race from window to window, barking uncontrollably.

If your dog has separation anxiety, and he panics and barks or howls every day when you leave him alone, his behavior will likely worsen. While you implement a behavior modification program, you'll need alternatives for your dog rather than leaving him home alone.

Taking him to doggie day care or to a friend or neighbor's house are options. You'll likely want to speak with your veterinarian about short-term medication. Medication alone does not resolve separation anxiety problems–it only helps behavior modification techniques work a bit better.

Avoid getting into the behavioral trap of giving your dog what he wants so he'll be quiet. This is a surefire, quick way for your dog to develop the bad habit of using noise to get what he wants.

3. Meet your dog's behavioral needs

Some barking problems develop because a dog's behavioral needs are not being met. Dogs need mental stimulation and social time with people. If your dog is spending long hours alone with little stimulation to exercise his physical body or his mind, he may bark to break the monotony and cope with his isolation. You may need to invest more time in giving your dog what he needs. More play time, more walks, even taking him to a training class may help break the monotony.

If your lifestyle necessitates your dog be left alone all day, again most evenings, and you don't have time for him on the weekends, perhaps it would be better for both you and your dog to find him another home.

Perhaps your dog wasn't well socialized and is barking because he is fearful of or aggressive toward people or even harmless, everyday events. You'll need to spend time in remedial socialization exercises by pairing things your dog is afraid of with something he loves, such as food or toys. You may need professional help from a qualified behaviorist to do this successfully.

However, there is another side to the coin. Some dogs, due to individual and/or breed tendencies, just seem to like to bark. These "reactive barkers" have a very low threshold for barking, and barking seems to be an enjoyable activity for them. Although significant variability exists within any breed, certain breeds are known for their tendency to vocalize. Examples include shelties, beagles, and many of the northern breeds that seem to enjoy howling.

Except for the "recreational barker," excessive barking is usually a symptom that a dog's welfare is compromised. As a responsible pet owner, it's your job to provide for your dog's behavioral needs.

4. Use the "Take-Away" Method for discouraging unwanted behavior

When our pets do things we don't like, whether it is barking or some other behavior, the first thought that comes to mind is, "How can I get him to stop?" Yet, when we think about suppressing behavior, we usually think of doing something unpleasant–anything from yelling to using a shock collar–to stop the dog from repeating the annoying behavior.

There is another way. Rather than administering something unpleasant, you can instead "take away" something your dog wants. If you have children, you may be familiar with this "take-away" or negative punishment technique. If your child brings home a bad report card, you might take away her phone privileges for a month. If your child comes home late from a date, you might say no dates for two weeks. You are negatively punishing undesirable behaviors (subtracting, taking away what your child wants). You can use a similar approach with your dog. "Bad" behavior results in the loss of "good" things.

How to make the "take-away" approach work: First, you must be able to determine what your dog wants when he barks; second, you must be able to control his access to it; and third, you must be able to take it away.

Let's say your dog is barking to get your attention. If you walk away and close yourself in the bathroom for a minute, you've taken away what your dog wants, that is, access to you. Rather than barking resulting in getting your attention, barking causes your dog to lose his chance to get your attention.

After a few minutes, return to your dog and if he is quiet, give him the attention he seeks. If you do this sequence quickly and consistently when your dog barks for attention, the behavior will stop.

This technique won't work if barking is its own reward, such as in compulsive barking or comfort-seeking barking. In these cases you cannot take away the dog's rewards for barking because they're internal.

In addition, the "take-away" method won't work well if you can't control the rewards for the behavior. For example, if your dog is territorially barking, he's been reinforced for it when people walk past your house. To your dog, his barking has caused the "intruders" to leave. It's not practical to have people stand in front of your house until your dog stops barking in order to remove the reward for the behavior!

5. Minimize "discipline" (positive punishment) and use it correctly when necessary

Whether you use the informal word, discipline, or the more technical term, positive punishment (adding something unpleasant), what is meant is any sort of unpleasant event you use to suppress your dog's barking.

Punishment should never be the first or only method you try to use to deal with your dog's barking. Be sure you've used some or all of the four preceding steps before resorting to discipline (positive punishment) to correct your dog's barking problem.

Punishment isn't always a good idea because it can sometimes create more problems than it solves. Any aversive event that successfully stops your dog's behavior has the potential to also trigger fearful or aggressive behavior.

If your attempts at punishment haven't worked, it may be that you aren't using punishment correctly. There are a number of requirements that must be met for any punishment to be used effectively and humanely. As you'll see, these requirements are often difficult to meet, which is why punishment must be used carefully. As you read through the following list, you'll see that anti-bark collars usually meet some of these requirements better than owner-delivered punishment. Let's look at some of the most important requirements.

• Punishment must be immediate

Let's say you hear your dog barking in the backyard. You run to the door and squirt your dog with water and he quiets down. You haven't punished your dog for starting to bark, but rather for barking longer than the 15 seconds it took you to get to the door to squirt him.

Your dog will react to his triggers, but as soon as he sees you pick up the squirt bottle, he'll stop barking. You've successfully interrupted your dog's barking once he starts, but you've not made it less likely he'll start barking in the first place. But being able to "turn off" your dog's barking sooner may be enough for you.

So, the first requirement for effective punishment is that it must happen as soon as your dog starts barking. Once your dog has revved himself into a real barking fit, it will be harder to stop him.

If you aren't there to discourage your dog from barking, you'll need other means to suppress the behavior. A remote device such as an anti-bark collar that delivers punishment the instant your dog starts barking, better meets the immediacy requirement. This leads to the second requirement for effective and humane punishment.

• Remote punishment is better

For several reasons, it's generally better if the punishment is remote rather than interactive (delivered by you). Remote punishers should be triggered automatically by your dog's behavior. Anti-bark collars are examples of remote punishers. Whether this type of collar is best for your dog will depend on the reason your dog is barking.

Most remote punishers deliver the same unpleasant consequence each and every time. With interactive punishment, what you do to discipline your dog may be quite variable. Sometimes you may yell loudly, other times you may softly ask your dog to be quiet. Variability in the intensity of punishment makes it less effective.

Remote punishment also disassociates you from the unpleasantness. Constantly yelling at your dog can damage your relationship. It's also unrealistic to think that you can be there to discipline your dog every time his barking needs to be curtailed. This relates to the third requirement for punishment–consistency.

• Punishment should be consistent

When your dog barks too much, if something unpleasant happens only part of the time and not every time, he'll likely play the odds and continue to bark. If you

determine that punishment must be used to be effective, it must be delivered every single time your dog barks to excess. Obviously, if you can't be present to suppress your dog's barking, you'll need to find some other way of doing it.

When used correctly, remote punishers such as anti-bark collars do a good job of meeting the requirements for consistency and immediacy. The pros and cons of remote anti-bark devices are discussed in Chapter Eight.

• Punishment should be unpleasant but not too unpleasant

The unpleasant event you choose as a punisher must be strong enough to make your dog want to change his behavior to avoid it, but not so strong that it causes excessive fear or pain. This is a fine line to walk. Even mild punishers, such as being squirted with water, cause some degree of anxiety or discomfort, otherwise your dog wouldn't stop what he's doing to avoid being squirted. Even these mild punishers can be used incorrectly. Repeatedly harassing your dog with "No, no, no!" to get your dog to stop barking without success also damages your relationship.

Punishment that is too strong can create generalized fear or aggression problems. It's never acceptable to hit or strike your dog. Improper use of anti-bark collars can cause dogs to be afraid to go outside or avoid other areas, because they associate the punishment from the collar with where they were when it was delivered.

• Limitations of punishment

Most importantly, punishment may suppress undesirable behaviors, but it never teaches your dog what he should be doing instead of barking. If you are going to use punishment to stop your dog's barking, you should also reward your dog for doing something else, such as sitting quietly or chewing on a toy.

Shannon Parish

Chapter Seven
What <u>To</u> Do About Your Dog's Barking: Using the Positive Proaction Plan© to Solve Barking Problems

This chapter will help you apply the **Positive Proaction Plan**© to the particular type of problem barking you identified from the **BarkCharts** in Chapter Five.

To better understand dog behavior, behaviorists have attempted to classify the reasons dogs bark into categories. These categories may overlap.

In any situation, dogs can have more than one reason to bark. For example, your dog may bark at visitors as a greeting, but also because she's frustrated at not being able to immediately get attention from your arriving guests. Or perhaps your dog barks at the delivery person because he's invaded her territory, but also because delivery people are frightening to your dog.

Your dog will reflect these mixed motivations by rapid changes in or combinations of body postures. For example, your dog may initially appear offensively threatening, with a deep bark as the delivery person first arrives. But as the person approaches her, your dog may choose to retreat, put her ears back, and shift to a higher pitched bark as she becomes more fearful or defensive.

Any of these categories of barking and other vocalizations can be socially facilitated. This means that your dog may vocalize simply because other dogs nearby are doing so, for whatever reason. Howling at sirens is a common example of socially facilitated noisemaking. One dog in the neighborhood starts and you can hear the howling progress house by house, block by block.

For each of the categories that follow, we have described how your dog should look and sound, and what motivates her behavior. Then, we have suggested options for addressing the problem based on the **Positive Proaction Plan**©. Not all of the options will work for your problem, but you should find some that you can use.

Be creative in applying the steps of the **Positive Proaction Plan**© to your dog's barking. Brainstorm with your family about additional things you can do to help your dog be quiet. Remember, focus on the first four steps of the Plan. If you decide punishment or discipline is needed, don't make it the first or only step you apply.

If you know or suspect that your dog is barking due to pain or medical causes, aggression, fear or separation anxiety, we strongly encourage you to seek professional help from a veterinarian and/or a qualified, experienced behavior consultant to address the problem. To do nothing can be dangerous to others and/or harmful to your dog.

If you don't have a behavior consultant in your area, visit **www.BarkingHelp.com** or **www.AnimalBehaviorAssociates.com** and consider a telephone or email consultation with us.

Aggressive vocalizations

Your dog may be barking and/or growling to warn or drive away people or animals from her territory. Your dog's territory may be small (the car for example) or large (the entire block) and have nothing to do with your property boundaries.

Children walking to school, joggers, bicyclists, delivery people, anyone coming to your door, on your street or in your building, loose dogs and cats, and even neighbors in their own yard, can all be perceived as territorial intruders and may trigger territorial barking. Your dog will be quiet when the "intruder" leaves. The behavior is reinforced if your dog believes she is driving away the intruder–"I bark and the mail carrier leaves!" You may have inadvertently contributed to the problem by allowing or encouraging "on patrol" behavior when your dog barks or growls at unfamiliar people, animals or noises.

Your dog may make similar sounds when she's being protective of people or other animals she views as part of her social group. If your dog believes the behavior of others is a threat to you, she may begin barking.

Your dog may misunderstand a person who is hugging you, dancing with you, wrestling with you, shaking your hand or handing you a package. Rather than being harmless behaviors, overly protective dogs may bark under these circumstances because they think you are being threatened.

If your dog is very fearful of a person or other animal, she may become defensively aggressive. This can happen when someone approaches your dog, reaches for her or tries to handle her and she feels she cannot get away.

Your dog will appear either offensively or defensively threatening when she's barking aggressively. It should also be clear what your dog is barking at.

Important points to remember about aggressive vocalizations:

- Your dog may bark and/or growl.

- Aggressive vocalization occurs on or near what your dog perceives to be her territory.

- It can occur whether family members are present or not, although it may be less frequent in your presence if you've corrected your dog for the behavior.

- Vocalizations are directed at people or other animals or, rarely, inanimate objects.

- Aggressive protective vocalizations are the same as territorial vocalizations except they occur when your dog is approached by another dog or person who is perceived to be a threat to her social group.

- Fearful dogs may become defensively aggressive when they feel trapped and cannot get away.

- The duration lasts only as long as the stimulus (person, dog or animal) is present.

- Your dog displays threatening behavior while vocalizing.

What to do :

- Your first and most important job is to protect people and other animals from your dog. Growling and aggressive barks are threats and should always be taken seriously. Keep your dog away from others except when you are sure you can control your dog's behavior and ensure everyone's safety. Your dog may need to be muzzled while you are working with her.

- When your dog isn't barking aggressively, reward her for her nonaggressive behavior.

- Teach your dog to be friendly to everyone by staging introductions so that people approach in a nonthreatening way and have either a treat or toy to give to your dog. You may need assistance from a qualified, experienced animal behavior consultant to help you stage these introductions successfully and safely. Don't try to do these exercises unless you can keep other people and animals safe.

- Don't allow aggressive vocalizations to become a habit. Don't permit "on patrol" behavior or allow your dog to be unfriendly to people she doesn't know. Remove your dog from the situation that is triggering her aggressive barking.

- Punishment that causes fear or pain may trigger further aggression.

- Before using an anti-bark collar on a dog that is barking aggressively, seek the advice of a qualified animal behavior consultant. The primary problem you need to work on is the aggression. The barking is only a symptom of this more dangerous problem. If you don't have a behaviorist in your area, visit **www.BarkingHelp.com** or **www.AnimalBehaviorAssociates.com** and consider a telephone or email consultation with us.

Alerting or greeting vocalizations

Barking, howling, whining, whimpering, yelping, and, rarely, growling, can all occur when your dog alerts you to some change in her world, such as a person coming near your house, or the arrival of a delivery or trash truck. Your dog's intent is not to drive the individual or object away, but rather just to let you know it is there.

Your dog's body postures and associated behaviors will help you distinguish between alert barking and aggressive barking. Refer back to the body posture section for specific details. Nearby neighborhood dogs often join in when one dog alerts to something. This is the common "neighborhood bark-fest" that often is heard in response to sirens or other noises.

Alerting barking can blend into greeting behavior as people, or perhaps other dogs, come to your door or fence. During greetings, your dog will usually appear friendly, playful and/or submissive. The noise making can escalate if you or others encourage this behavior (or at least don't discourage it), or if the behavior results in pleasant social interactions for your dog.

Greetings can become chaos at the door if arrivals become a production and your dog receives attention from you and others when she's barking and out of control. See the Resources Available From Animal Behavior Associates in Chapter Ten of the book for help with this problem.

Important points to remember about alerting or greeting vocalizations:

- Your dog may bark, howl, whine, whimper, yelp or growl. If the dog is very excited, the yelping can be very high-pitched, almost sounding as if your dog is in pain.
- Alerting vocalizations can occur any time of day or night, anywhere.
- These vocalizations are elicited by the approach of a person or dog, when greeting people or dogs, or when something has changed in the environment.
- Your dog shows alerting, friendly, playful or submissive body postures.

What to do:

- Reward your dog for not barking when greeting others or when alerted.

- Teach your dog to come to you and sit quietly when she hears or sees something, rather than bark while racing around the house or yard. Tidbits will help in this training.

- Give your dog something else to do to replace the barking behavior when she greets people. If your dog loves playing fetch, have your guests toss a ball or other favorite toy a few times for your dog when they first arrive. It's hard to bark with a ball in your mouth. Plus, this helps your dog work out some of her excited energy so she can better control herself and be quiet.

- Change the environment to keep your dog away from situations that trigger barking. You may need to block her access to certain rooms where she can see out the window. If she's jumping on furniture or windowsills to see out, discourage her by covering them with plastic carpet runners, pointy side up. Consider closing draperies or blinds, or putting up a secondary barrier to keep your dog from seeing through the fence.

- Limit your dog's unsupervised access in the yard if she is spending much of her day engaging in "on-patrol" barking.

- When your dog barks excessively, give her a brief "time-out" (a few minutes) by confining her someplace she doesn't want to be until she is quiet. A small, dog-proofed bathroom works well.

- Use a water bottle or loud noise to interrupt the barking, then give your dog something else to do. Have her sit or give her a chewie.

- Anti-bark devices can be used in conjunction with other methods, or if other methods are unsuccessful.

Playful vocalizations

When dogs play they may make a variety of sounds including barks, yelps, whines, whimpers or growls. Dogs make these sounds when they are together in a backyard, or if they see one another through a fence.

The sounds your dog makes either elicit play behavior from others or are part of the play itself. For example, your dog may bark or whine to entice you to play with her, or as two dogs are playing, they may bark or growl at each other.

Dogs show friendly body and play postures such as the play bow. Jumping up on or pawing the other dog or person is common.

Important points to remember about playful vocalizations:

- Your dog barks, whines, whimpers, yelps or growls.

- Playful vocalizations are directed toward people, other animals or sometimes inanimate objects, such as balls or other toys.
- They are not related to a particular time of day or to family presence.
- Playful body postures accompany vocalizations.

What to do:

- Encourage games and play in which your dog is less likely to bark. If your dogs can play tug with each other quietly, be sure to provide plenty of tug toys. If your dog becomes noisy when playing tug with you, play fetch instead.
- Don't encourage your dog to bark by teasing her, or playing keep-away with her toys.
- If a play bout becomes loud and noisy, end the game by either taking away the toy or giving your dog a time-out. As long as the dog is quiet, play can continue.
- If you want to allow noisy playtimes, take your dog to other locations to play where her barking won't be an issue.
- Anti-bark devices can be used carefully in conjunction with other methods or if other methods are unsuccessful.
- If you are trying to suppress barking that occurs when two dogs are playing in your absence, be aware that using an anti-bark shock collar can cause one dog to aggressively attack the other when shocked.

Attention-seeking vocalizations

Your dog may bark, whine, whimper or yelp in order to get attention or something else she wants from people or other animals. Dogs often bark to get attention when their owners are otherwise occupied, such as talking on the phone. Your dog may whine or bark at the back door because doing so usually causes you to let her inside.

Even "negative attention" such as yelling at your dog, may be reinforcing, causing the behavior to continue. This is most likely to happen if your dog isn't receiving enough attention from you, or if she hasn't been taught other, more appropriate behaviors to get your attention.

If barking causes you to give your dog what she wants, then barking is working for your dog and will continue. If your dog is barking to get attention, her body postures may vary but are usually friendly. You may also see your dog jumping up, or pawing or nudging you as part of the attention-seeking sequence.

Important points to remember about attention-seeking vocalizations:

- Your dog barks, whines, whimpers or yelps.
- Attention-seeking vocalizations are directed at people or animals or places where these individuals are (e.g., at the house if your dog is in the yard).
- They usually occur when your dog is by herself in a particular location but people or animals are in close proximity.
- They occur whenever your dog wants attention and has learned that being noisy will work for her.
- They are accompanied by friendly or playful body postures.
- They are associated with other behaviors such as jumping up, scratching, digging or pawing.

What to do:

- Teach your dog to sit quietly instead of bark to get your attention.
- You can teach your dog to paw at a bell hung on the door when she wants to be let in or out, as a replacement for barking.
- Temporarily avoid situations, places or things that trigger the barking. For example, you might let your dog inside before she starts barking at the door.
- Remove the reward for the behavior. If your dog barks at you so you'll play with her, get up and walk away or leave the room instead. If your dog brings you a toy and waits quietly, play with her.
- Ignore your dog until she stops barking. Expect her to bark louder and longer at first before she learns this won't work to get what she wants.
- Anti-bark devices can be used carefully in conjunction with other methods or if other methods are unsuccessful.

Comfort-seeking and boredom vocalizations

This category describes dogs that are vocalizing because they are socially isolated in a boring environment without much to do. These dogs aren't getting their behavioral needs met and could be described as neglected "backyard" dogs. Comfort-seeking and boredom vocalizations are different from attention-seeking vocalizations because they occur when no one is around to attend to the dog.

Attention-seeking barking has been rewarded at some point. Comfort-seeking vocalizations such as barking, whining, howling, whimpering or yelping are more of your dog's attempt to cope with an inadequate environment.

With either comfort-seeking or boredom vocalizations, your dog may not be barking at anything, because there is nothing there to bark at! Or she may direct her vocalizations toward areas where people are likely to be, even though no one is around.

There may not be any remarkable body posture features to see as these dogs are vocalizing. Their features may appear fairly neutral and at ease, or you might see some signs of fear or anxiety.

Important points to remember about comfort-seeking and boredom vocalizations:

- Your dog is not getting her behavioral needs met and may be neglected.
- Your dog is attempting to cope with isolation and/or a barren and uninteresting environment.
- Your dog displays neutral or anxious body postures.
- She doesn't appear to bark at anything, or she may bark at an unoccupied house, garage or car.

What to do:

- Give your dog more stimulating toys to play with. Interactive toys stuffed with treats that your dog has to work out are a good choice. A selection of these toys is available at **www.BarkingHelp.com** or **www.AnimalBehavior-Associates.com** and from other wholesalers and retailers.
- Spend more time with your dog. Play with her, take her to a training class, give her more walks or take her with you when you go visiting or run errands.
- Give your dog access to other friendly dogs to provide social stimulation. Set up "play dates" with neighborhood dogs or take her to a doggie day care.
- If your dog is kept primarily outside, allow her more time inside. Consider a doggie door.
- If your dog is crated for long periods of time, transition her to not need the crate. Modify destructive or housesoiling behavior with help from a qualified, experienced animal behavior consultant.
- Hire a dog walker or pet sitter to give your dog an exercise break if you will be away from home for long hours on a daily basis.
- Anti-bark devices can be used carefully in conjunction with other methods or if other methods are unsuccessful. Do not use anti-bark devices as a substitute for taking better care of your dog and meeting her needs.

Fear/distress/anxiety vocalizations

If your dog is afraid of specific noises such as thunderstorms or fireworks, she may bark, whine, whimper, yelp, scream or growl when she hears those sounds. For example, thunderphobic dogs may bark or yelp during high winds or thunderstorms.

When dogs are threatened in social interactions with people or other dogs, they may also vocalize.

If your dog has had several frightening experiences in the same place, such as the backyard, she may connect the fear to that location and may bark there even in the absence of the original trigger. Thunderphobic dogs may bark or howl whenever they are outside in the spring or summer even if it's not storming, because the outside has become a scary place to be.

Dogs barking for these reasons will display fearful or submissive body postures and/or may try to escape or hide from the feared event or stimulus. They may destructively paw, dig or chew at the fence or house. If you've confined your dog to a crate to prevent this destructiveness, your dog will likely also try to escape from the crate. Injuries from these attempts are not uncommon.

Important points to remember about fear/distress/anxiety vocalizations:

- Your dog barks, whines, whimpers, yelps, screams or growls.
- The vocalization is associated with the presence of a fear producing stimulus (at least initially).
- It is accompanied by other fearful behavior such as hiding, avoidance and fearful or submissive body postures.
- The vocalization is not dependent on family's presence, although some dogs may react more intensely to the feared stimulus when alone.
- If the behavior has generalized, it can continue for a long duration even in the absence of the stimulus.

What to do:

- Good socialization during puppyhood and ongoing socialization experiences into adulthood can go a long way in preventing these problems.
- Once you identify what's triggering your dog's reaction, help your dog associate "good things" with the events or people that frighten her. For example, make sure every new person your dog meets offers her a treat or a toy.
- Create "practice sessions" that are similar to the events that frighten your dog, but not as intense. Then pair the "good things" with this less intense

trigger. Don't continue these sessions if your dog isn't getting better or if she gets worse. You may need the help of a qualified, experienced animal behavior consultant to help you do this successfully. If you don't have a behaviorist in your area, visit our Web site at **www.BarkingHelp.com** or **www.Animal-BehaviorAssociates.com** and consider a telephone or email consultation with us.

- Temporarily protect your dog from being around the things that frighten her, unless you are with her to provide the "good things" mentioned above. If your dog is thunderphobic for example, let her come inside the house. If you can create a sound-dampening room for her to be in, even better.

- Talk to your veterinarian about possible short-term medications to reduce your dog's fear, distress or anxiety.

- Crating or confinement in small areas to prevent destructive behavior or housesoiling that is sometimes associated with fear and anxiety is NOT appropriate. Doing so can either make your dog more fearful, or cause her to hurt herself attempting to break out of the confinement.

- Any sort of punishment including anti-bark devices, is NOT appropriate with dogs that are fearful or anxious. Trying to punish fearful reactions will only make your dog more fearful or cause her to show her fear in other ways.

Separation anxiety vocalizations

As social animals, being left alone is a significant source of stress for many dogs. Dogs can become anxious or distressed when separated from anyone (person or animal) to whom they are attached.

Barking, howling, whining, whimpering or yelping that begins usually within 30 minutes of your departure are manifestations of separation anxiety. Your dog may bark at the door from which you departed or the windows from where she can see you, or not direct her vocalizing at anything in particular.

Another common symptom of separation anxiety is destructive behavior directed at doors, windows and household or personal items that have your scent, such as couch cushions or your clothing. Housesoiling that occurs only in your absence is also associated with separation anxiety.

These behaviors not only begin within the first 30 minutes after your departure, but occur consistently whenever your dog is left alone. It's common for separation anxiety dogs to "shadow" or follow people around the house, be depressed or anxious when you leave, and/or show frantic greetings when you return.

Dogs with separation anxiety have frequently been obtained from humane societies or found as strays, and become strongly attached to their owners or other family animals. A recent change in the dog's ownership, a change in family work schedules, a move to a new home, a recent vacation during which the dog was left home alone (with regular caretaker visits) or boarded, or death of another pet or person can all trigger separation anxiety problems. This is one of the most common causes of problem vocalizations that occur only when dogs are left alone.

Important points to remember about separation-anxiety vocalizations:

- Your dog barks, whines, whimpers, yelps or screams.
- These vocalizations occur only when your dog is separated from her owners or others to whom she is attached.
- They can occur when your dog is inside the house, outside in the yard, or less commonly, when left alone in a vehicle.
- They occur consistently when alone, or with a particular pattern of absences, such as occurring only in the evenings.
- They begin within the first 30 minutes after departure.
- They may be accompanied by destructiveness, escape attempts, urination/defecation.
- Your dog displays fearful or anxious body postures.
- Your dog is not barking at anything, or may appear to be barking toward doors, windows, gates.
- Your dog follows you excessively, shows distressed departure reactions, or shows frantic greetings.

What to do:

- Teach your dog the coping skills she needs to be calm and relaxed when left alone. You will need to teach your dog different behaviors in reaction to your departure routine and absences from the house, as well as decreasing her need to follow you around when you are home. Behavior modification for separation anxiety requires many, many repetitions and strict attention to detail. You will likely need help from a qualified, experienced animal behavior consultant to help you create a specific plan for your dog. If you don't have a behavior consultant in your area, visit our Web site at **www.BarkingHelp.com** or **www.AnimalBehaviorAssociates.com** and consider a telephone or email consultation with us.

- Keep arrival and departure routines very low-key. Don't get your dog all excited about your comings and goings because this makes your absences more difficult for her to tolerate.

- If at all possible, avoid leaving your dog alone. Each panic attack makes it harder to change her behavior. Consider doggie day care, taking her to work with you (if circumstances permit), or leaving her with a friend or neighbor. Some dogs are better if left indoors rather than outside.

- Talk to your veterinarian about possible medications to reduce your dog's anxiety while you implement a behavior modification plan. Medication by itself will not solve separation anxiety problems.

- Crating or confining your dog to prevent destructive behavior or housesoiling that is sometimes associated with fear and anxiety is NOT a good choice. Doing so can either make your dog more fearful or cause her to hurt herself attempting to break out of the confinement.

- Because separation anxiety is really a fear-based problem, any sort of punishment, including anti-bark devices, typically increases your dog's anxiety and causes her to express her anxiety in other ways. If circumstances (such as threatened eviction) force you to resolve the barking problem rapidly, consult an experienced behavior consultant for advice about whether punishment can be carefully incorporated into a complete behavior modification plan.

Painful or medically caused vocalizations

Dogs that are ill, injured or in pain may whine, whimper, yelp or scream. They may also growl or bark, especially in response to attempts to touch and handle the injured or painful body part. This type of vocalization can also be elicited by punishment that elicits pain.

Vocalizations may be accompanied by body postures characteristic of pain. These include fearful body postures, hiding, or attempts to protect the painful area by curling up, not moving, limping, etc. But dogs in chronic pain may not vocalize at all.

Important points to remember about painful or medically caused vocalizations:

- Your dog whines, whimpers, yelps, screams or rarely, barks or growls.

- Your dog may be injured or ill.

- The vocalizations may also be in response to remote or owner-delivered punishment.

- They aren't dependent on a specific location or whether family members are present.
- Your dog shows fearful or painful body postures.
- Your dog may hide or try to protect a body area.
- Your dog may also pace, circle, limp or show other signs of injury.

What to do:

- Identify the cause of the pain and remove it (for example, loosen a collar that is too tight).
- If you cannot identify or protect your dog from the source of the pain, or if your dog seems sick, take her to your veterinarian for medical evaluation and treatment.
- Stop any punishment that is triggering these vocalizations. If you are using an anti-bark device that is causing your dog to cry out or yelp repeatedly, either discontinue its use or choose a lower intensity, or seek help from an experienced behavior consultant.
- Never punish your dog after the fact, that is, once the "bad" behavior has stopped.

Frustration vocalizations

Your dog may bark, yelp, whine, whimper or howl if prevented from "doing what she wants to do." For example, a dog may bark at a squirrel on top of the fence that she cannot reach or at children playing across the street that she is prevented from joining.

Your dog will appear alert and the vocalizations are often accompanied by attempts to engage in the prevented behavior, such as jumping up, pawing at restraints or fences, pacing, circling, etc.

Important points to remember about frustration vocalizations:

- Your dog barks, whines, whimpers, yelps or howls.
- Your dog is attempting to engage in another behavior or accomplish a goal, e.g., digging under the fence to play with another dog, jumping up to catch a squirrel or cat on top of the fence.
- Your dog barks at someone or something.
- Your dog may continue for long time periods if she continues to be frustrated.

- No fearful behavior is seen.
- Frustration vocalizations may be accompanied by a variety of body postures including play or an alert posture.

What to do:

- Identify the source of the frustration (what does your dog want but can't get to?).
- Teach your dog how to cope with her frustration by giving her other things to do. For example, if she is barking at your children playing in the yard, give her a special interactive toy or chewie to occupy her.
- Remove your dog's source of frustration by changing her environment. Close the drapes or put your dog in another room so she can't see the children playing across the street. If your dog barks at squirrels all day, let her spend part of the day inside.
- Crating or confining your dog where she can still see what she wants, but can't get to it, will only increase her frustration, and therefore, is not an option.
- If you try to suppress your dog's barking with any sort of punishment, including anti-bark devices, you may only increase her frustration. However, using an anti-bark device while also giving your dog something else to do may be helpful.

Compulsive vocalizations

Compulsive barking occurs repetitively, without interruption, for long periods of time, and is very difficult to interrupt. There may not be any apparent trigger, or the dog may compulsively bark at everyday sights and sounds.

Dogs have been known to compulsively bark at the telephone ringing, the sound of a toaster popping up, or light reflections and shadows. The dog seems oblivious to things around him.

The barking may be accompanied by other repetitive behaviors such as pacing, spinning or circling. This is similar to the compulsive behavior shown by people. These behaviors require help from both a veterinarian and a qualified behavior consultant.

Important points to remember about compulsive vocalizations:

- Your dog barks, howls, yelps or growls.

- Your dog may bark at nothing, or the barking may be triggered by specific events.

- Compulsive vocalizations may happen whether family is present or not.

- They can continue for long periods.

- Your dog is not fearful, frustrated or threatening.

- Your dog seems oblivious to things around her.

- This behavior is difficult to interrupt.

What to do:

- Compulsive behaviors can often be influenced by physiological conditions. Take your dog to your veterinarian for medical evaluation and treatment. Medications may be helpful in reducing this type of barking.

- Try teaching your dog to do something else in response to the events that trigger her barking. If your dog barks compulsively at trash trucks, use irresistible tidbits to keep her lying down when she hears the truck. You may need help from a qualified, experienced animal behavior consultant to help you stage training situations to successfully accomplish this. If you don't have a behavior consultant in your area, visit our Web site at **www.BarkingHelp.com** or **www.AnimalBehaviorAssociates.com** and consider a telephone or email consultation with us.

- Keep your dog away from situations, places or things that trigger the barking. You may be able to keep your dog inside to prevent her from barking at trash trucks.

- Avoid crating or confining your dog in small areas where she is still exposed to her triggers for barking. This may create more problems. However, if you can confine your dog in an area away from her triggers, this may be helpful.

- Use any sort of punishment, including anti-bark devices, only under the direction of a qualified, experienced animal behavior consultant. Using such devices incorrectly for compulsive barking creates a great risk of developing other problems.

"Beware of silent dogs and still waters."

– Portuguese proverb

Chapter Eight
Anti-bark Devices and Surgical Debarking

Anti-bark devices

There are a variety of remote and/or automatic devices to choose from that punish dogs when they bark. The automatic devices, usually some form of collar, have the advantage of meeting most of the criteria for effective punishment. They deliver punishment immediately, consistently, at a chosen intensity, in your absence, and only when your dog barks (if used and operated correctly). The devices use a variety of aversive stimuli, some of which are more effective than others.

When an anti-bark device functions correctly and is the right choice for your dog, your dog's barking should be quickly suppressed without your dog becoming excessively fearful or upset. When punishment is used correctly, it should only be necessary to deliver it a few times (some behaviorists recommend 3-5 repetitions). Thus, dogs should only be subjected to the aversive event from a collar a relatively small number of times. If your dog continues to bark despite the punishment from the collar, then either the device is being used incorrectly or it is not the right choice for your dog.

Cautions on the use of anti-bark devices

As a general rule, punishment and anti-bark devices should not be used for barking problems that are motivated by pain, illness, compulsions, aggression, fear or separation anxiety. As you've already learned, punishment doesn't address the underlying motivation, and may create additional problems, even if the barking decreases.

We do not believe punishment or any anti-bark device should be used as the only method to resolve barking problems. Under the right conditions, anti-bark devices can be a useful part of a complete behavior modification plan that is rich in rewards and takes into account the dog's behavioral needs. Read this book carefully to help you decide whether an anti-bark device is right for your dog. If you need more information, we recommend you consult with a qualified, experienced behavior consultant or visit our Web sites–**www.BarkingHelp.com** or **www.AnimalBehaviorAssociates.com**.

When first using any of these collars, it is imperative that you both follow the manufacturer's instructions and closely observe your dog's response. Never put the collar on and immediately leave the house. You need to know how your dog is responding to the collar and whether you need to make adjustments in the fit or intensity of shock or sound. Currently, the amount of spray delivered by a spray collar cannot be adjusted.

Collars that use sound as punishment

These collars emit either audible or ultrasonic sound (above the hearing range of people but not dogs) to punish barking. These sound-making collars may be aversive to some dogs, but not all. Some dogs may find the noise sufficiently unpleasant at first to stop barking, but most dogs habituate or adapt to the noise and resume barking. We don't generally recommend them. They are less expensive than shock or spray collars, but are generally less effective.

Scented spray collars

When we recommend anti-bark devices, this is the kind of collar we often start with. The Premier Gentle Spray™ collar sprays a mist of dilute citronella oil while the PetSafe Spray Bark Control™ uses a lemon fragrance to stop barking. The companies that developed these collars maintain they work because they affect three of the dogs' senses: the dogs hear the spray, smell the spray and feel the spray. Studies show that spray collars are more effective than sound collars and just as effective as shock collars for the majority of dogs.

The spray collars rarely elicit aggression or fear. Under careful supervision from a qualified, experienced behavior consultant, spray collars can be used as part of a behavior modification plan even for aggressively motivated barking. In fact, one citronella product, Direct Stop© (see order form at the back of this book) is often used to discourage aggressive behavior. We do not recommend you use spray collars for this type of barking problem without professional assistance.

If you've decided an anti-bark device is appropriate for your dog, but a spray collar has been ineffective at stopping your dog's barking, you can consider a shock collar.

Shock collars

Electric shock is almost always aversive enough to stop most dogs from barking. For a variety of reasons, a small percentage of dogs continue barking in spite of the shock.

You have several brands of shock collars to choose from. Some brands say they deliver a harmless electrical stimulation, negative static correction, unpleasant sensation, static electric impulse or a correction. Regardless of what the manufacturers call it, the dog receives an electrical shock.

If you decide to use one of these collars, choose one that allows you to adjust the intensity of the shock for the body weight, pain sensitivity and motivational level of your dog.

For the average dog, we recommend you start with a middle range shock intensity. If your dog has a low pain threshold and is particularly sensitive or timid, you might want to start at the lowest, or second lowest intensity. For dogs with high pain thresholds or when sound or spray collars have been ineffective it may be better to start one level above mid-range.

Be careful about starting too low and having to gradually increase the shock intensity. It is possible to condition your dog to tolerate higher and higher levels of shock with this approach.

Several companies manufacture shock collars. Several of the most well known and readily available are made by PetSafe™, Innotek™ and Tritronics™.

Chapter Ten provides information about obtaining these and other anti-bark devices.

Remote devices other than collars

Another type of remote device is a small box containing a microphone that is placed someplace near the barking dog. When the sensor detects the sound of the dog's bark, it emits a loud screech or ultrasonic noise in response. The device will reset automatically and can be triggered repeatedly. It can also be triggered manually by pressing a button on the top of the device.

Like the sound collars, they seem to work for some dogs. Unfortunately, these devices can sometimes be triggered by sounds other than barking. Their advantage is that neighbors can use them by either placing the device near the fence, or triggering it manually when the dog barks.

The PetSafe™ Premium Ultrasonic Bark Control, the Innotek Ultrasonic™ , and the Sure-Stop Barker Breaker™ from Amtek are three examples. See Chapter Ten for information about obtaining these devices.

Devocalization

Surgical debarking may be a last resort for some dog owners. It should only be considered if all other strategies have failed and euthanasia is the only other option. Debarking doesn't result in a silent dog, however. The dog is still able to make a rasping-type noise, but it may not be loud enough to carry very far.

Scar tissue can develop around the vocal chords and the resulting sound can be even more annoying and disturbing than barking. Devocalization also does nothing to decrease the dog's motivation to bark.

Most methods of devocalization are considered major surgery that requires general anesthesia. This is not risk-free for the dog and can be expensive. A newer method called ventriculochordectomy - oral approach is much less invasive and reported to have fewer complications. Talk with your veterinarian about these surgical procedures.

Some people consider surgical debarking cruel. However, there have been no objective studies to determine if debarking results in other behavior changes or behavior problems.

The American Veterinary Medical Association has taken the following position on this procedure: *"Canine devocalization should only be performed by qualified, licensed veterinarians as a final alternative after behavioral modification efforts to correct excessive vocalization have failed."*

Chapter Nine
Guidelines for Choosing a Dog Trainer
or Behavior Consultant

As we've mentioned, you may sometimes need professional help to resolve your dog's barking problem. How do you know who to call? Do you need a dog trainer or a behavior consultant? What's the difference? How do you choose one or the other from the pages and pages of listings in the telephone book?

What do dog trainers do?

A dog trainer works with you to teach your dog specific skills such as sitting when told, coming when called, and walking on a leash without pulling. Trainers often give advice or educate you about other training issues such as jumping up, crate training, or adjusting your dog's manners around other people and dogs.

Trainers generally instruct you how to train your dog and supervise your training. Some trainers at board-and-train facilities will train your dog themselves, without you being present. We don't generally recommend this approach. While the trainer may be able to train your dog to behave well at his facility, getting your dog to behave for you at home is another thing entirely. Some trainers work with other animals such as cats or horses, and do behavior consulting as well.

Expect to pay a fee for both training classes and individual, private training. Prices vary widely depending on where you live and the expertise and quality of the trainer.

What do behavior consultants do?

A behavior consultant is a person who works with you to manage, resolve or prevent specific behavior problems you may be having with your pet. These may include things such as aggression, fears and phobias, separation anxiety, or housesoiling. These are not "obedience" problems, and training classes or private training instruction won't help them.

Behavior consultants identify the cause of the problem and then recommend a plan for you to implement to change the behavior. Consultants both tell you and show you what to do, but generally do not take your dog and work with her for you.

Behavior consultants may work with dogs, cats, or other species such as horses or birds. Some behavior consultants also perform dog training.

Behavioral consultants use a variety of professional titles, including applied animal behaviorist, animal behaviorist, behavior specialist, dog psychologist, behaviorist, or veterinary behaviorist. Because veterinarians are regulated by law, only board certified veterinarians may use the title veterinary behaviorist or veterinary behavior specialist. Anyone, regardless of training or experience, can use the other titles.

Behavior consultants also charge a fee for their services. Don't expect free advice, tips, or solutions in "25 words or less."

Where to find trainers and behavior consultants

You'll find both dog trainers and behavior consultants listed in the telephone book or local pet publications. Rather than taking your chances in the phone directory, you are better off asking for a referral from your veterinarian or local animal shelter.

You can also find lists of certified pet dog trainers, certified applied animal behaviorists, and certified veterinary behaviorists from the Web sites listed in the Web section of Chapter Ten.

What does certification mean?

Quite a few new "certification" groups have appeared in the last few years, many of which are merely "certifying" graduates of their own training programs or schools. This type of certification has no validity or credibility and is not representative of a true professional certification. If someone says they are "certified," you should ask:

a. What group or organization does the certification come from? Credible certification programs are administered by independent professional organizations without ties to any specific training program or school.

b. What are the criteria for certification? Credible certification programs should not require individuals to be graduates of any specific training program or school. Look for educational, experiential and ethical criteria, as well as required letters of recommendation, testing, and/or professional review of the individual's work.

c. Is the certifying group associated with a training school or program? Credible certification programs are not associated with the program that trains the certificants.

Certifications for behavior consultants

Academically trained behavior consultants can be certified by the Animal Behavior Society (ABS) or the American College of Veterinary Behaviorists (ACVB). The requirements for certification and a list of certified consultants can be found on the organizations' Web sites, which are listed in the Web section of Chapter Ten.

Certification for dog trainers

The Certification Council for Pet Dog Trainers (CCPDT) certifies dog trainers. The CCPDT works with an independent testing agency to administer a qualifying examination. The requirements for certification and a list of certified trainers can be found at the CCPDT's Web site. See the Web site section in Chapter Ten.

Tips for evaluating dog trainers and behavior consultants*

✪ Ask trainers from where and what type of training they received to become a professional trainer, how long they've been training professionally, and what kind of experience they have. Ask behavior consultants how they acquired their knowledge about behavior, and how they learned to be a behavior consultant. Look for academic training in animal learning and ethology, as well as supervised practical training.

✪ Look for both trainers and behavior consultants who hold memberships in professional organizations and who pursue continuing education. This indicates individuals who are interested in keeping current on the latest advances in their field.

✪ Both dog trainers and behavior consultants are really educating and training you, so look for people with good communication and social skills, whom you feel comfortable talking to. Look for professionals who treat both people and dogs with respect and compassion. ABS, AVMA and the APDT all have ethical statements and guidelines on their Web sites.

✪ Choose trainers and behavior consultants who focus on encouraging and rewarding the right behavior with positive reinforcement, rather than relying on punishing or correcting undesirable ones. Both professionals should be willing to use whatever type of positive reinforcement works best for your dog, whether it is food, toys, petting or all three.

✪ Look for trainers who recognize the importance of you working with your own dog under their direction, rather than sending your dog somewhere for a professional trainer to train. Problem behavior often won't be manifested during a behavior consulting appointment (e.g., housesoiling), so it's up to you to work with your dog by following through with the recommendations given by the behavior consultant.

✪ Avoid anyone who guarantees results. Dogs are living creatures and no one knows enough about their behavior to guarantee outcomes. Some trainers and behavior consultants may guarantee satisfaction with their professional services, which is different.

✪ Observe a training class without your dog. Are the dogs and people enjoying themselves? Talk to participants to see if they are comfortable with the training methods used. If a trainer won't let you sit in on a class, don't enroll. If, for confidentiality reasons, you are unable to observe a behavior consultation involving another pet owner, ask the behavior consultant for references, such as from veterinarians or shelters that use their services, or from former clients who have given permission to share information.

✪ Basic dog training can be accomplished without the use of choke chains, so don't enroll in a class that requires one. Head collars, buckle collars, and even certain types of harnesses are better choices.

✪ If either a trainer or behavior consultant tells you to do something to or with your dog that you don't feel comfortable with – don't do it! Don't be intimidated, bullied or shamed into doing something that you believe is not in the best interest of your dog. Don't allow anyone to work directly with your dog unless they first tell you what they are going to do. Don't be afraid to tell any trainer or behavior consultant to stop if they are doing something to your dog that you don't like.

✪ Because behavior problems can have medical causes, look for behavior consultants who encourage you to first consult with your veterinarian. Even if your pet doesn't look or act sick, medical conditions can affect your dog's behavior. Be wary of trainers or behavior consultants who insist on diet or other nutritional changes without relying on input from your veterinarian. Only veterinarians can prescribe medication for your dog.

✪ No matter how good the trainer or behavior consultant is, if you don't follow through with practice either in your everyday life with your dog, or with special practice sessions, you won't get the results you desire.

✪ The Delta Society publishes a booklet entitled, *Professional Standards for Dog Trainers: Effective, Humane Principles*, which provides guidance in identifying humane and effective dog training principles. It is available from their Web site listed in the Web site section of Chapter Ten. Look for trainers who follow these principles.

* Modified from an article by S. Hetts in *The Advocate*, 1996, The American Humane Association, and from S. Hetts, *Pet Behavior Protocols: What To Say, What To Do, When To Refer*, 1999, AAHA Press.

Chapter Ten
References and Resources

References

Adams, G. J. & Clark, W. T. 1986. *The prevalence of behavioural problems in American dogs.* Modern Veterinary Practice, 67: 28-31.

Beaver, B. V. 1994. *Owner complaints about canine behavior.* Journal of the American Veterinary Medical Association, 204: 1953-1955.

Fox, M.W. 1987. *The Dog: Its Domestication and Behavior.* Malabar, FL: Krieger Publ. Co., 69-89.

Juarbe-Diaz, S.V. & Houpt, K.A. 1996. *Comparison of two anti-barking collars for the treatment of nuisance barking.* Journal of the American Animal Hospital Association, 32: 231-235.

Juarbe-Diaz, S.V. 1997. *Assessment and treatment of excessive barking in the domestic dog.* Veterinary Clinics of North America: Small Animal Practice, 27(3): 515-532.

Landsberg, G. M. 1991. *The distribution of canine behavior cases at three behavior referral practices.* Veterinary Medicine, October: 1011-1018.

Simpson, B.S. 1997. *Canine communication.* Veterinary Clinics of North America: Small Animal Practice, 27(3): 445-464.

Vacalopoulos, A. & Anderson, R. K. 1992. *Canine behavior problems reported by clients in a study of veterinary hospitals.* Paper presented at the annual meeting of the American Veterinary Medical Association, Boston, MA.

Voith, V. L. 1985. *Analysis of 2,500 telephone calls about behavior problems of dogs and cats.* Paper presented at annual meeting of the Animal Behavior Society, Raleigh, NC.

Yen, S. 2002. *A new perspective on barking dogs.* (Canis familiaris). Journal of Comparative Psychology, 116(2): 189-193.

Yen, S. & McCowan, B. 2004. *Barking in domestic dogs: context specificity and individual identification.* Animal Behaviour, 68: 343-355.

Bark control products available from Animal Behavior Associates at
www.BarkingHelp.com

Direct Stop™ Animal Deterrent Spray $18.95

Uses the same citronella spray as the anti-bark collar. Comes in hand-held spray container, which is an alternative if for some reason a collar isn't possible. Can also be used to stop animal attacks and fighting among animals, or to deter nuisance wildlife.

PetSafe™ Comfort-Fit Deluxe Bark Control Collar PBC00-10678 $109.95

Eighteen levels of self-adjusting correction, durable, waterproof receiver with adjustable Quick Fit™ buckle.

PetSafe™ Premium Deluxe Bark Control Collar PDBC-300 $99.95

Three correction modes, each with six levels of Static Correction that automatically adjust to your dog's temperament.

PetSafe™ Premium Spray Bark Control Collar PSBC-300 $109.99

Uses a safe, natural lemon scent to deter barking.

PetSafe™ Premium Ultrasonic Bark Control PBC-1000-19 $39.95

Not a collar but a hand-held or mounted device that emits an ultrasonic sound to deter barking. Sensor responds automatically when barking sounds are detected, or can be activated manually.

Premier Gentle Spray™ Citronella Anti-bark Collar $109.95

The collar sprays a harmless mist of citronella oil every time the dog barks.

Books and booklets available from Animal Behavior Associates at
www.BarkingHelp.com [Contact us for quantity pricing]

Additional copies of this book ***Help! I'm Barking and I Can't be Quiet*** $19.95
This innovative book helps owners identify the causes of barking and devise strategies to solve them.

What Dogs Need and How They Think   **$5.50 each**
76 Ways to Get Your Dog to Do What You Want

These 16-page booklets are packed with useful tips on how to make your relationship with your dog the best it can be.

You'll learn:
- Why it's a good idea to drop a tidbit when you walk by your resting dog
- Why you should ignore annoying behaviors from your dog
- You don't need to bully your dog to get him to do what you want
- Why every dog needs a private place away from the family

Raising a Behaviorally Healthy Puppy: A Pet Parenting Guide   **$15.95**
What you do during your puppy's first 4 months of life will have a lasting and sometimes unchangeable impact on your dog's adult behavior. This book gives you the critical knowledge you need to make the most out of these formative months.

Inside you'll find our unique Five Step Positive Proaction Plan© for dealing with major puppy issues from housetraining to getting along with other pets. In an easy to read format you'll learn:

- How to evaluate your puppy's behavioral health
- How to best socialize your puppy
- How to meet your puppy's behavioral needs
- Alternatives to "discipline" and saying "NO" over and over
- What's important and what's not when it comes to "dominance"
- A step by step guide to crate training
- And much, much more

Suitable both for puppy parents and for trainers, veterinarians, and shelters to distribute in their puppy classes.

Managing Chaos at the Door   **$12.95**
Listen to Drs. Hetts and Estep give you over ten different strategies to use when the doorbell rings and your dog goes berserk. This audio CD plays on any CD player or your computer.

Other Resources Available from Animal Behavior Associates, Inc.

Sign up TODAY at our Web site for "**Pet Behavior One Piece at a Time**"

Full of indispensable information on pet behavior, our **FREE** newsletter will help you be the pet parent your pet deserves.

A variety of helpful and educational resources and products are available through our Web site **www.AnimalBehaviorAssociates.com**. Free, downloadable articles discuss the causes and possible solutions to a variety of behavior problems.

"Canine Body Postures"   **$50.95**

A 45-minute videotape that describes the communicative behavior of dogs–how to read dog behavior signals, recognize fearful and aggressive behavior, and influence the behavior of dogs. Also available in DVD format.

"Dog Bite Prevention Training Program"   **$299.00**

A 60-minute VHS or DVD education program for anyone who goes on property where there may be dogs. Shows how to recognize the signs of dogs on a property, how to recognize dangerous dogs, and what to do to avoid injury by dogs. A complete education system with printed workbooks and testing materials for training groups of home service providers.

"Just Behave: How to Get Your Dog to Do What You Want"   **$29.95**

This two-hour live telecourse, complete with 13 pages of class notes, is a must for every dog owner. Both your dog's behavior and your relationship with your pet will improve when you take this course. You'll learn:

- What a behaviorally healthy dog is and how to have one
- Why thinking your dog is rebellious, spiteful or jealous can hurt your dog and your relationship
- A five step plan to prevent and manage ANY behavioral issue you have with your dog
- How to prevent problems by meeting your dog's behavioral needs
- Much, much more!

Check our Web site, **www.AnimalBehaviorAssociates.com**, call or email for upcoming dates.

Bark control products available from other sources

Bark Limiter XS™. Available from TriTronics Inc., P. O. Box 17660, Tucson, AZ 85731; 800-456-4343, www.tritronics.com.

Innotek Ultrasonic Trainer. Available from Drs. Foster & Smith, P.O. Box 100, Rhinelander, WI 54501; 800-826-7206, www.DrsFosterSmith.com.

The Sure-Stop Barker Breaker. Available from Drs. Foster & Smith and PETsMART stores and the PETsMART catalog. 1989 Transit Way, Box 910, Brockport, NY 14420; 800-872-3773, www.PETsMART.com.

Web sites mentioned in this book

The Animal Behavior Society	www.animalbehavior.org
The Association of Pet Dog Trainers	www.apdt.com
The Certification Council for Pet Dog Trainers	www.ccpdt.org
The Delta Society	www.deltasociety.org (Go to the online store)
Diplomates of The American College of Veterinary Behaviorists	www.dacvb.org

ORDER FORM

Listed below are the products mentioned in this book, and other products you might find useful.
These products and more can be purchased through our secure shopping cart at
www.AnimalBehaviorAssociates.com
You may also order by phone at **303.932.9095**
or by faxing this completed Order Form to **303.932.2298**
or by mailing this completed Order Form to **4994 S. Independence Way, Littleton CO 80123**

Product	Price	Quantity	Total
Direct Stop™ Animal Deterrent Spray	$ 18.95		$
PetSafe™ Comfort-Fit Deluxe Bark Control Collar PBC00-10678	109.99		
PetSafe™ Premium Deluxe Bark Control Collar PDBC-300	99.95		
PetSafe™ Premium Spray Bark Control Collar PSBC-300	109.99		
PetSafe™ Premium Ultrasonic Bark Control PBC-1000-19	39.95		
Premier Gentle Spray™ Citronella Anti-bark Collar	109.95		
Help! I'm Barking and I Can't Be Quiet: A Pet Parenting Guide	19.95		
What Dogs Need and How They Think	5.50		
76 Ways to Get Your Dog to Do What You Want	5.50		
Raising a Behaviorally Healthy Puppy: A Pet Parenting Guide	15.95		
Managing Chaos at the Door	12.95		
Canine Body Postures	50.95		
Dog Bite Prevention Training Program	299.00		
Just Behave – Telecourse (no S&H)	29.95		
		Subtotal	$
	Colorado residents only: Add 3.5% sales tax		
Shipping and handling charges: Orders up to $19.00 = $3.00 Orders from $19.01 to $150.00 = $7.00 Orders over $150.01 = $10.00 (Do not include telecourse when calculating shipping charges)			$
		GRAND TOTAL	$

Credit Card: ❏ [MasterCard]   ❏ [VISA]

Name as it appears on card: _____

Credit card number: _____

Expiration date: _____ / _____

Your signature: _____

❏ Check enclosed. Make payable to **Animal Behavior Associates, Inc.**

Ship to: Name_____

Address_____

City/St/Zip_____

Questionnaires and Checksheets

The following pages contain two complete sets of the questionnaires, worksheets and flowcharts that have been referenced throughout this book.

For your convenience, on pages 97-108 you will find a perforated set of these checksheets that you can easily tear from the book for your use.

My Dog's Barking Profile

Try to answer all the questions in this **Profile**. The more information you have, the more successful you will be at identifying why your dog is barking and finding the right solution. Your dog's barking problem may have more than one cause. Check all the boxes that apply.

1. What is your dog doing? ❏ Barking ❏ Howling
   ❏ Whining/whimpering ❏ Yelping ❏ Growling ❏ Screaming

   What kind of emotion do you think your dog has when he barks?
   Does he sound: ❏ Happy ❏ Excited ❏ Threatening ❏ Fearful
   ❏ In pain ❏ Don't know

2. What does your dog look like when he is barking?
   ❏ Looks or acts friendly ❏ Looks or acts offensively threatening
   ❏ Looks or acts defensively threatening ❏ Looks or acts fearful
   ❏ Looks or acts playful ❏ Looks or acts alert ❏ Paces, circles, limps,
   hides, looks ill or in pain ❏ Don't know

3. Where is your dog barking? ❏ Inside house ❏ In a fenced yard
   ❏ In unfenced area of property ❏ When tied on rope/chain
   ❏ When running free or at large ❏ When in a vehicle ❏ When on
   leash walks ❏ When he is prevented from getting to other dogs,
   people or things ❏ When isolated from other people or dogs or when
   he is in a barren environment ❏ When he is at other locations
   Explain : _____

4. When does the barking occur?
   Days of the week _____
   Time of day _____
   ❏ When someone is home ❏ When no one is home
   ❏ Only when left alone or when he is separated from people.

   If it occurs when no one is home, does it begin within a half hour after
   your dog is separated from people? ❏ Yes ❏ No

   If it occurs at certain times or on certain days of the week, are there
   specific things happening at those times that may cause the barking
   (such as the mail delivery person arriving)? ❏ Yes ❏ No
   If yes, what is happening? _____

My Dog's Barking Profile – page 2

5. How consistent is the barking in this (these) location(s) and time(s)?
    ❏ Almost every time ❏ Better than half the time
    ❏ Less than half the time ❏ Very erratic, occurs rarely

    Is there a consistent pattern to the barking? ❏ Yes ❏ No

6. Is your dog barking at something? ❏ Yes ❏ No, appears to bark at nothing. If yes, go to question 7, if no, skip to question 9.

7. What is your dog barking at? ❏ Your family members ❏ Other people ❏ Other dogs ❏ Other animals (cats, squirrels, birds, etc.)

8. What is your dog barking at? ❏ Inanimate moving objects (vehicles, hot air balloons, thunderstorms, the wind) ❏ Inanimate stationary objects (house, parked cars, trees, rocks, etc.) ❏ Other
    Explain:_____

9. When your dog barks, does he seem oblivious to everything around him and difficult to interrupt? ❏ Yes ❏ No

10. What else does your dog do when he is barking? ❏ Scratches or digs at doors, windows, gates or fences ❏ Chews or bites at doors, windows, gates or fences ❏ Urinates or defecates ❏ Destroys other things (clothes, furniture, etc.) ❏ Other behavior
    Explain:_____

11. How does your dog act when you leave and return?
    Does he act agitated, anxious, fearful or depressed when people get ready to leave home? ❏ Yes ❏ No

    Is he overly excited when you return home? ❏ Yes ❏ No

    Does he follow you around excessively when you are home?
    ❏ Yes ❏ No

12. Other relevant information and notes:

    _____

    _____

    _____

    _____

My Dog's Body Posture Checklist

Record your observations. Put a check mark next to the elements you observe when your dog is barking.

My dog's overall body carriage

- ❑ Stiff legs, upright stance
- ❑ Upright stance, not stiff
- ❑ Crouched
- ❑ Body weight shifted to forequarters
- ❑ Body weight shifted to hindquarters
- ❑ Sitting or lying down
- ❑ Directly facing what he's barking at
- ❑ Turned away or hiding from what he's barking at
- ❑ Moves toward what he's barking at
- ❑ Moves away from what he's barking at
- ❑ Play bows

My dog's ear carriage

- ❑ Ears pricked forward or upright
- ❑ Ears pulled back against head or bent down to the side
- ❑ Variable, may be upright or slightly back
- ❑ Cropped ears

My dog's tail carriage

- ❑ Tail straight up or high
- ❑ Tail carried low, straight out and/or pointing downward
- ❑ Tail tucked between legs
- ❑ Tail stationary, not moving
- ❑ Tail wagging furiously and rapidly from side to side
- ❑ Tail wagging slowly and deliberately from side to side
- ❑ Variable, may be slightly lowered or held high
- ❑ Docked or no tail

My Dog's Body Posture Checklist – page 2

My dog's eyes and gaze

- ❑   Dog staring directly at what he's barking at
- ❑   Dog looks away from a direct stare, avoids eye contact
- ❑   Eyes open normally, soft without a hard stare
- ❑   Eyes wide open, whites of eyes exaggerated
- ❑   Pupils (center black part of eye) dilated

My dog's facial expression

- ❑   Mouth closed and relaxed
- ❑   Mouth open but relaxed
- ❑   Baring teeth by retracting lips vertically (up and down) from the front of the mouth. Canine teeth mostly visible
- ❑   Baring teeth by retracting lips horizontally from the corners or back of the mouth. Molars or side teeth visible
- ❑   Snaps or tries to bite
- ❑   Teeth not showing but muzzle tense and/or puckered
- ❑   Submissive grin

Are My dog's hackles up? (Piloerection or erect hair)

- ❑   Yes
- ❑   No
- ❑   Partly

Key to My Dog's Body Postures

(Use this information to answer Question 2 on **My Dog's Barking Profile**.)

Interpret your observations. Put a check mark in the box next to the characteristic you checked on the **Checklist**. Go through all the descriptions below and check the appropriate boxes.

Offensive threats (Figure 1)

Dogs threaten to warn others to go away or stop what they are doing. Threatening dogs may or may not escalate to biting. Dogs who are offensively threatening are not afraid. They are demonstrating their willingness to initiate a conflict or fight, and may move or lunge toward their opponent. The body postures associated with offensive threats make the dog appear larger and more intimidating. Offensively threatening dogs can show one or more of the following:

Figure 1. Offensively threatening

© Courtesy ASPCA.

- ❏ 1. Stands tall with a stiff body posture
- ❏ 2. Body weight may be shifted to the forequarters so the dog is ready to lunge forward
- ❏ 3. May lunge, snap at, or chase others
- ❏ 4. Tail straight up, it may be wagging slowly and deliberately
- ❏ 5. Ears up and forward
- ❏ 6. Direct eye contact or staring
- ❏ 7. Teeth bared from the front of the mouth (vertical retraction of lips)
- ❏ 8. Teeth may not be showing but muzzle may be tense or puckered
- ❏ 9. Snaps or tries to bite
- ❏ 10. Hackles up

Defensive threats (Figure 2)

The defensive dog is both threatening and afraid. While such dogs are still warning others to stay away, they aren't interested in initiating a conflict. If left alone, they usually won't bite or attack. The body postures associated with defensive threats serve to make the dog appear smaller and less of a target. Defensively threatening dogs will show one or more fearful postures (1-6) **and** one or more threatening postures (7-10):

Figure 2. Defensively threatening

© Courtesy ASPCA.

- ❏ 1. Crouched or lowered body posture
- ❏ 2. Dog may shift body weight more to the rear quarters, as though leaning away from the opponent

Key to My Dog's Body Postures – page 2

- ❏ 3. May move away from opponent
- ❏ 4. Ears laid back or down
- ❏ 5. Tail straight out, down, or even tucked between the legs, not wagging
- ❏ 6. Dog usually looks away from a direct stare
- ❏ 7. Teeth bared from the back of the mouth (horizontal retraction of lips)
- ❏ 8. Teeth may not be showing but muzzle may be tense and/or puckered
- ❏ 9. Snaps or tries to bite
- ❏ 10. Hackles may be up

Fearful or submissive behavior (Figures 3 and 4)

Dogs can be fearful without being threatening. Submissive and fearful behaviors overlap with each other. Dogs show submission only during social interactions, but can show fearful behaviors toward sounds and objects as well. Fearful or submissive dogs can show one or more of the following:

Figure 3. Submissive or fearful

© Courtesy ASPCA.

- ❏ 1. Crouched body posture, or lying down, even rolled over on the back exposing the belly
- ❏ 2. May run away, or try to avoid the other person, or the fearful event or stimulus
- ❏ 3. Ears laid back or down
- ❏ 4. Tail down or tucked between the legs
- ❏ 5. Looks away and avoids direct eye contact
- ❏ 6. Eyes wide open, whites of eyes exaggerated
- ❏ 7. May retract the lips into a submissive grin
- ❏ 8. Mouth may be open but relaxed

Figure 4. Submissive

© Courtesy ASPCA.

Alert or orienting behavior (Figure 5)

When something catches your dog's attention, his body posture changes from being relaxed to being focused or directed to something specific. He's not yet decided whether to be friendly, fearful or threatening–he's just paying attention. Dogs who are alerting can display one or more of the following:

Figure 5. Alert or orienting

© Courtesy ASPCA.

- ❏ 1. Upright body posture, but usually not as stiff as the offensive dog–he may even be lying down
- ❏ 2. Body and gaze directed at the "thing" that has captured his attention
- ❏ 3. Ears upright

Shannon Parish

Key to My Dog's Body Postures – page 3

- ❑   4.   Tail variable, may be down or held high
- ❑   5.   Eyes open normally without a hard stare
- ❑   6.   Mouth open and relaxed or closed and relaxed

Friendly behavior

Surprisingly, friendly behavior is a little difficult to describe. Friendly dogs indicate a willingness to interact and they solicit attention. They may show elements of submission and play as well. Friendly dogs can show one or more of the following:

- ❑   1.   Body posture relaxed, not stiff-legged, may be slightly crouched or lowered
- ❑   2.   Moves towards the person or other dog
- ❑   3.   Variable ear carriage–may be upright or slightly back
- ❑   4.   Variable tail carriage–may be slightly lowered or held high, usually not tucked
- ❑   5.   If the tail is wagging, it should be a relaxed, yet rapid wag, not slow and deliberate
- ❑   6.   Eyes will appear "soft," without a hard stare
- ❑   7.   Mouth may be open or closed but is relaxed
- ❑   8.   May show other elements of submissive behavior
- ❑   9.   May lick, nudge or sniff people's hands or arms

Playful behavior (Figure 6)

Playful, friendly, and submissive behaviors often have elements in common. Dogs may show friendly behaviors in conjunction with or preceding playful behavior. Playful dogs can show one or more of the following:

- ❑   1.   A play bow
- ❑   2.   May paw at play partner
- ❑   3.   Variable ear carriage–may be upright or slightly back
- ❑   4.   Variable tail carriage–may be slightly lowered or held high, usually not tucked
- ❑   5.   Other friendly behaviors that alternate with threats and submissive behavior

Figure 6. Playful

© Courtesy ASPCA.

Once you have filled out the **Key to My Dog's Body Postures**, transfer this information to Question 2 of **My Dog's Barking Profile**. In general, the behavioral category with the most check marks is the one that best describes your dog's behavior when barking. If your dog appears to have several motivations at the same time, that is, you have more than one category with more than one check mark, enter all the interpretations that apply.

BarkCharts

Chart 1

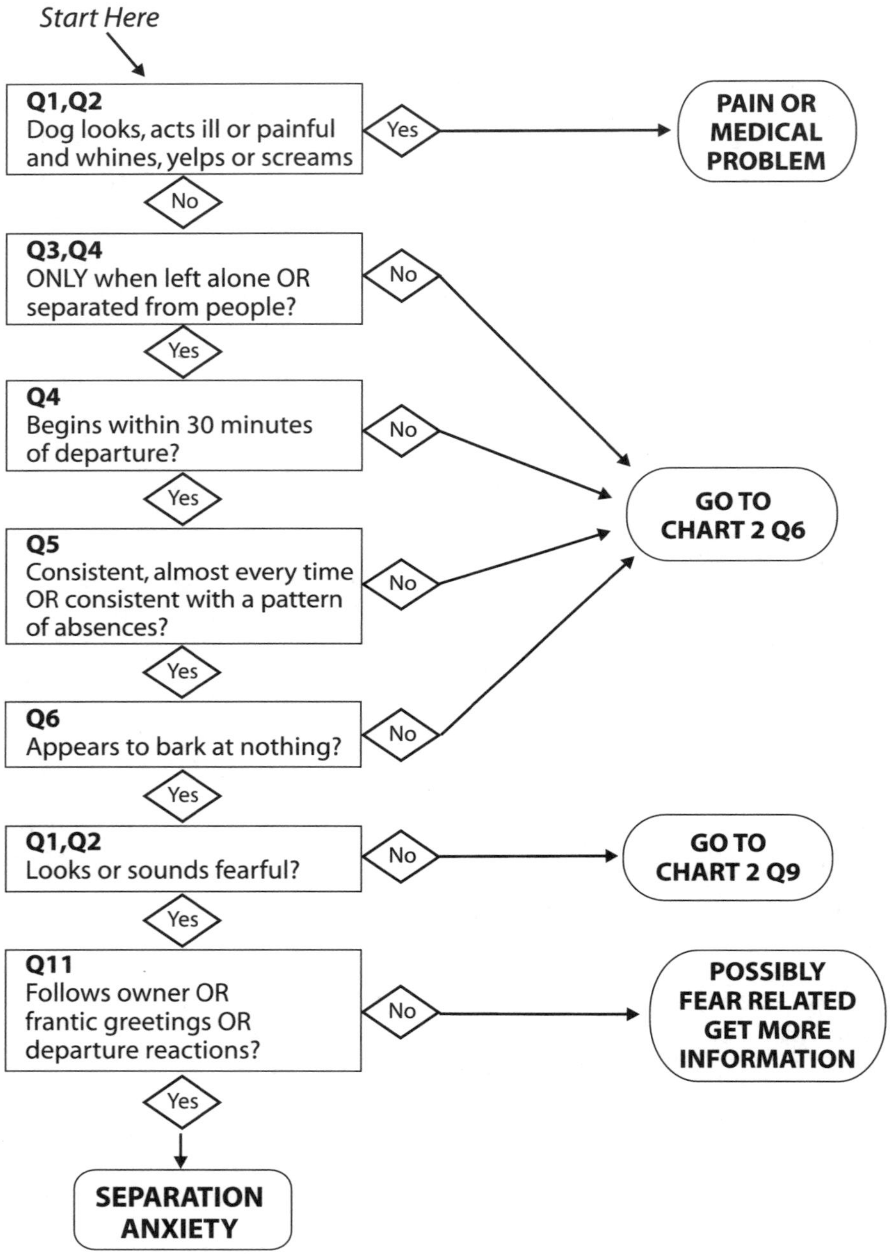

Start Here

Q1, Q2
Dog looks, acts ill or painful and whines, yelps or screams — Yes → **PAIN OR MEDICAL PROBLEM**

No ↓

Q3, Q4
ONLY when left alone OR separated from people? — No → **GO TO CHART 2 Q6**

Yes ↓

Q4
Begins within 30 minutes of departure? — No → **GO TO CHART 2 Q6**

Yes ↓

Q5
Consistent, almost every time OR consistent with a pattern of absences? — No → **GO TO CHART 2 Q6**

Yes ↓

Q6
Appears to bark at nothing? — No → **GO TO CHART 2 Q6**

Yes ↓

Q1, Q2
Looks or sounds fearful? — No → **GO TO CHART 2 Q9**

Yes ↓

Q11
Follows owner OR frantic greetings OR departure reactions? — No → **POSSIBLY FEAR RELATED GET MORE INFORMATION**

Yes ↓

SEPARATION ANXIETY

BarkCharts

Chart 2

Complete Chart 1 first

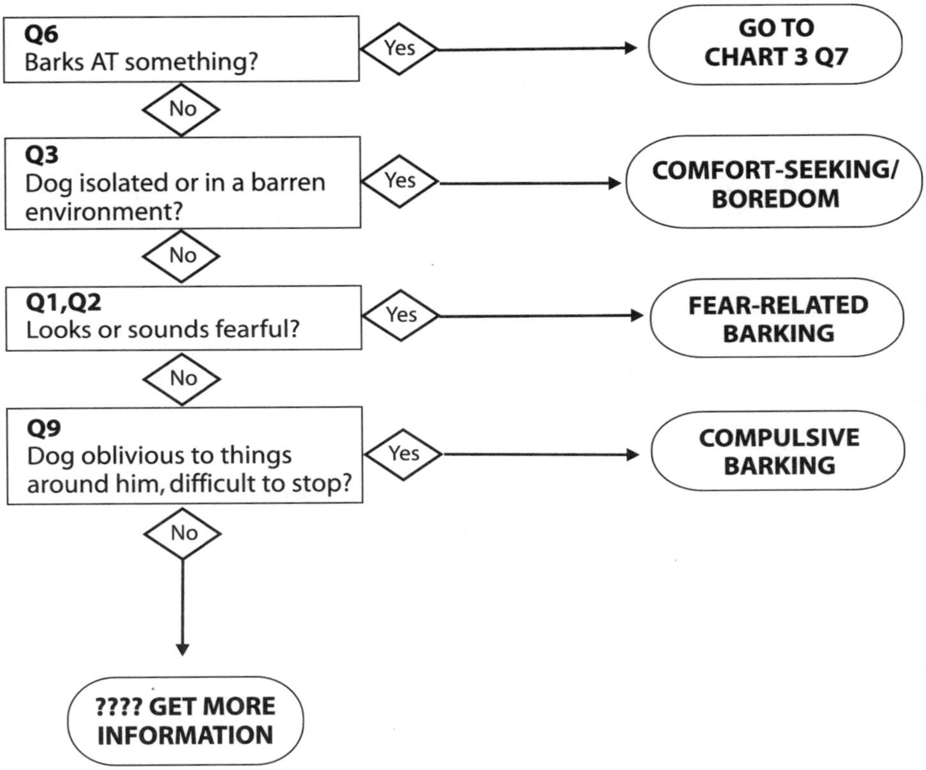

Q6
Barks AT something? — Yes → **GO TO CHART 3 Q7**

No

Q3
Dog isolated or in a barren environment? — Yes → **COMFORT-SEEKING/ BOREDOM**

No

Q1, Q2
Looks or sounds fearful? — Yes → **FEAR-RELATED BARKING**

No

Q9
Dog oblivious to things around him, difficult to stop? — Yes → **COMPULSIVE BARKING**

No

???? GET MORE INFORMATION

BarkCharts

Chart 3

Complete Chart 1 first

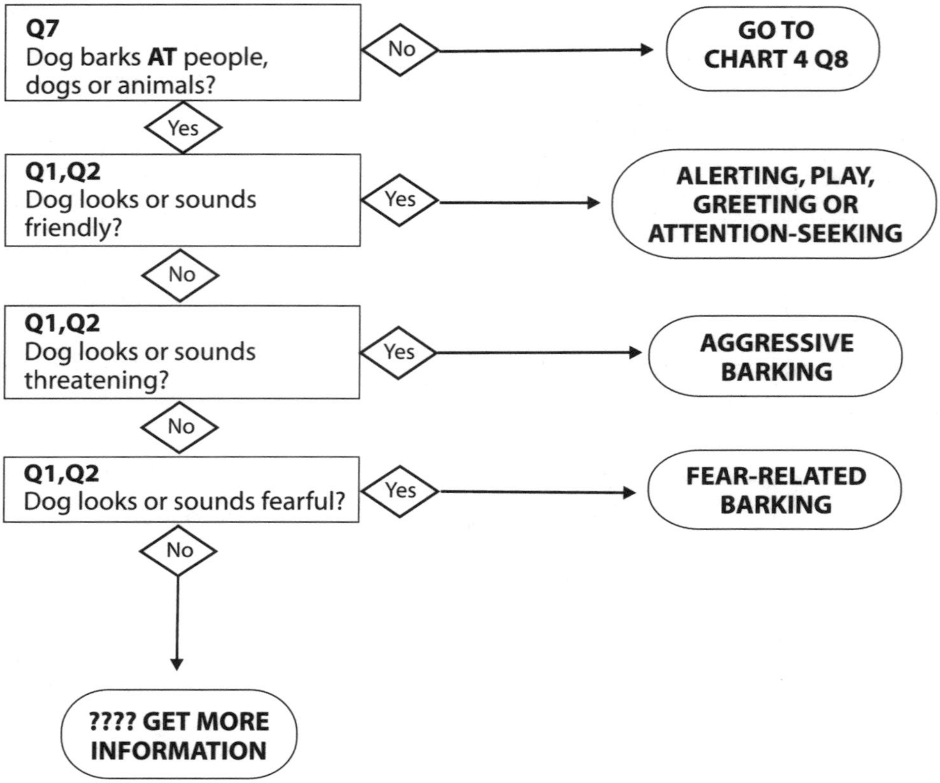

Q7
Dog barks **AT** people, dogs or animals? — No → **GO TO CHART 4 Q8**

Yes ↓

Q1,Q2
Dog looks or sounds friendly? — Yes → **ALERTING, PLAY, GREETING OR ATTENTION-SEEKING**

No ↓

Q1,Q2
Dog looks or sounds threatening? — Yes → **AGGRESSIVE BARKING**

No ↓

Q1,Q2
Dog looks or sounds fearful? — Yes → **FEAR-RELATED BARKING**

No ↓

???? GET MORE INFORMATION

BarkCharts

Chart 4

Complete Chart 1 first

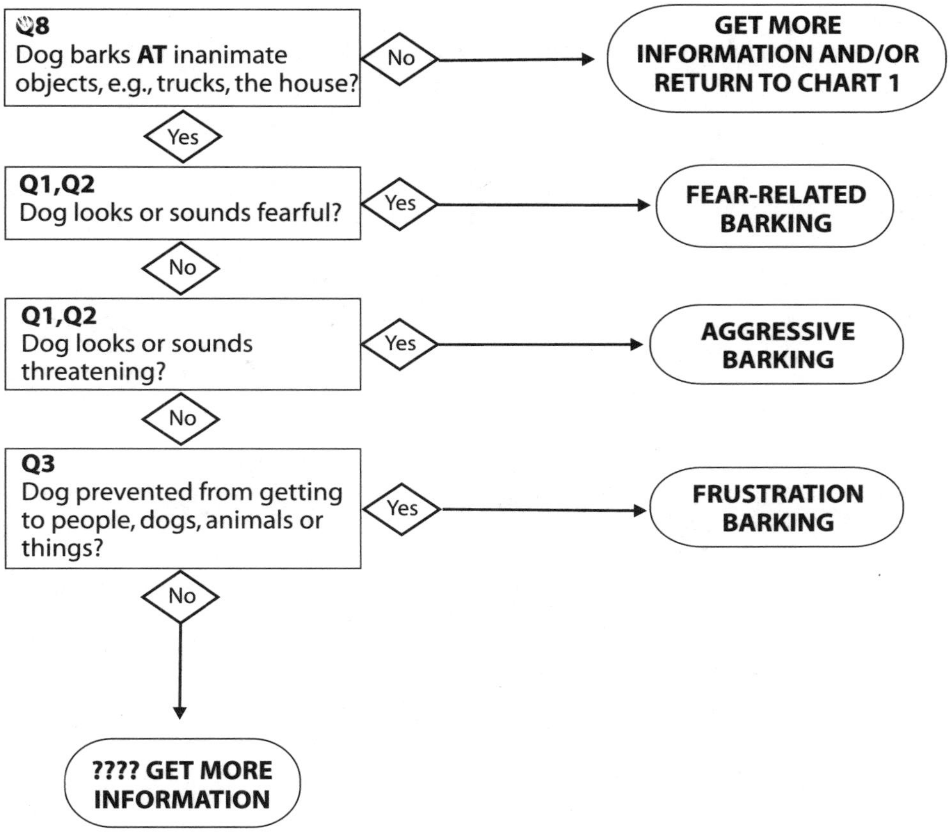

☺8
Dog barks **AT** inanimate objects, e.g., trucks, the house?

— No → **GET MORE INFORMATION AND/OR RETURN TO CHART 1**

Yes ↓

Q1,Q2
Dog looks or sounds fearful?

— Yes → **FEAR-RELATED BARKING**

No ↓

Q1,Q2
Dog looks or sounds threatening?

— Yes → **AGGRESSIVE BARKING**

No ↓

Q3
Dog prevented from getting to people, dogs, animals or things?

— Yes → **FRUSTRATION BARKING**

No ↓

???? GET MORE INFORMATION

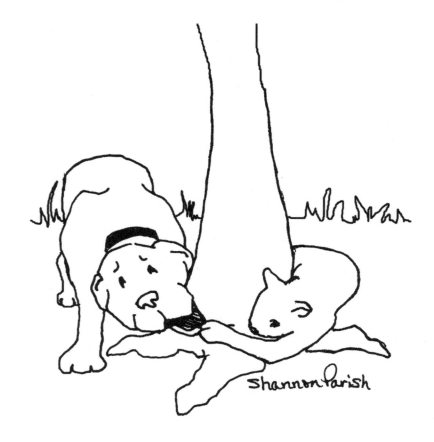

My Dog's Barking Profile

Try to answer all the questions in this **Profile**. The more information you have, the more successful you will be at identifying why your dog is barking and finding the right solution. Your dog's barking problem may have more than one cause. Check all the boxes that apply.

1. What is your dog doing? ❏ Barking ❏ Howling
   ❏ Whining/whimpering ❏ Yelping ❏ Growling ❏ Screaming

   What kind of emotion do you think your dog has when he barks? Does he sound: ❏ Happy ❏ Excited ❏ Threatening ❏ Fearful ❏ In pain ❏ Don't know

2. What does your dog look like when he is barking?
   ❏ Looks or acts friendly ❏ Looks or acts offensively threatening
   ❏ Looks or acts defensively threatening ❏ Looks or acts fearful
   ❏ Looks or acts playful ❏ Looks or acts alert ❏ Paces, circles, limps, hides, looks ill or in pain ❏ Don't know

3. Where is your dog barking? ❏ Inside house ❏ In a fenced yard
   ❏ In unfenced area of property ❏ When tied on rope/chain
   ❏ When running free or at large ❏ When in a vehicle ❏ When on leash walks ❏ When he is prevented from getting to other dogs, people or things ❏ When isolated from other people or dogs or when he is in a barren environment ❏ When he is at other locations
   Explain : _____

4. When does the barking occur?
   Days of the week _____
   Time of day _____
   ❏ When someone is home ❏ When no one is home
   ❏ Only when left alone or when he is separated from people.

   If it occurs when no one is home, does it begin within a half hour after your dog is separated from people? ❏ Yes ❏ No

   If it occurs at certain times or on certain days of the week, are there specific things happening at those times that may cause the barking (such as the mail delivery person arriving)? ❏ Yes ❏ No
   If yes, what is happening? _____

My Dog's Barking Profile – page 2

5. How consistent is the barking in this (these) location(s) and time(s)?
    ❑ Almost every time ❑ Better than half the time
    ❑ Less than half the time ❑ Very erratic, occurs rarely

    Is there a consistent pattern to the barking? ❑ Yes ❑ No

6. Is your dog barking at something? ❑ Yes ❑ No, appears to bark at nothing. If yes, go to question 7, if no, skip to question 9.

7. What is your dog barking at? ❑ Your family members ❑ Other people ❑ Other dogs ❑ Other animals (cats, squirrels, birds, etc.)

8. What is your dog barking at? ❑ Inanimate moving objects (vehicles, hot air balloons, thunderstorms, the wind) ❑ Inanimate stationary objects (house, parked cars, trees, rocks, etc.) ❑ Other
    Explain:_____

9. When your dog barks, does he seem oblivious to everything around him and difficult to interrupt? ❑ Yes ❑ No

10. What else does your dog do when he is barking? ❑ Scratches or digs at doors, windows, gates or fences ❑ Chews or bites at doors, windows, gates or fences ❑ Urinates or defecates ❑ Destroys other things (clothes, furniture, etc.) ❑ Other behavior
    Explain:_____

11. How does your dog act when you leave and return?
    Does he act agitated, anxious, fearful or depressed when people get ready to leave home? ❑ Yes ❑ No

    Is he overly excited when you return home? ❑ Yes ❑ No

    Does he follow you around excessively when you are home?
    ❑ Yes ❑ No

12. Other relevant information and notes:

    _____

    _____

    _____

    _____

My Dog's Body Posture Checklist

Record your observations. Put a check mark next to the elements you observe when your dog is barking.

My dog's overall body carriage

- ❑ Stiff legs, upright stance
- ❑ Upright stance, not stiff
- ❑ Crouched
- ❑ Body weight shifted to forequarters
- ❑ Body weight shifted to hindquarters
- ❑ Sitting or lying down
- ❑ Directly facing what he's barking at
- ❑ Turned away or hiding from what he's barking at
- ❑ Moves toward what he's barking at
- ❑ Moves away from what he's barking at
- ❑ Play bows

My dog's ear carriage

- ❑ Ears pricked forward or upright
- ❑ Ears pulled back against head or bent down to the side
- ❑ Variable, may be upright or slightly back
- ❑ Cropped ears

My dog's tail carriage

- ❑ Tail straight up or high
- ❑ Tail carried low, straight out and/or pointing downward
- ❑ Tail tucked between legs
- ❑ Tail stationary, not moving
- ❑ Tail wagging furiously and rapidly from side to side
- ❑ Tail wagging slowly and deliberately from side to side
- ❑ Variable, may be slightly lowered or held high
- ❑ Docked or no tail

My Dog's Body Posture Checklist – page 2

My dog's eyes and gaze

- ❏ Dog staring directly at what he's barking at
- ❏ Dog looks away from a direct stare, avoids eye contact
- ❏ Eyes open normally, soft without a hard stare
- ❏ Eyes wide open, whites of eyes exaggerated
- ❏ Pupils (center black part of eye) dilated

My dog's facial expression

- ❏ Mouth closed and relaxed
- ❏ Mouth open but relaxed
- ❏ Baring teeth by retracting lips vertically (up and down) from the front of the mouth. Canine teeth mostly visible
- ❏ Baring teeth by retracting lips horizontally from the corners or back of the mouth. Molars or side teeth visible
- ❏ Snaps or tries to bite
- ❏ Teeth not showing but muzzle tense and/or puckered
- ❏ Submissive grin

Are My dog's hackles up? (Piloerection or erect hair)

- ❏ Yes
- ❏ No
- ❏ Partly

Key to My Dog's Body Postures

(Use this information to answer Question 2 on **My Dog's Barking Profile**.)

Interpret your observations. Put a check mark in the box next to the characteristic you checked on the **Checklist**. Go through all the descriptions below and check the appropriate boxes.

Offensive threats (Figure 1)

Dogs threaten to warn others to go away or stop what they are doing. Threatening dogs may or may not escalate to biting. Dogs who are offensively threatening are not afraid. They are demonstrating their willingness to initiate a conflict or fight, and may move or lunge toward their opponent. The body postures associated with offensive threats make the dog appear larger and more intimidating. Offensively threatening dogs can show one or more of the following:

Figure 1. Offensively threatening
© Courtesy ASPCA.

- ❑ 1. Stands tall with a stiff body posture
- ❑ 2. Body weight may be shifted to the forequarters so the dog is ready to lunge forward
- ❑ 3. May lunge, snap at, or chase others
- ❑ 4. Tail straight up, it may be wagging slowly and deliberately
- ❑ 5. Ears up and forward
- ❑ 6. Direct eye contact or staring
- ❑ 7. Teeth bared from the front of the mouth (vertical retraction of lips)
- ❑ 8. Teeth may not be showing but muzzle may be tense or puckered
- ❑ 9. Snaps or tries to bite
- ❑ 10. Hackles up

Defensive threats (Figure 2)

The defensive dog is both threatening and afraid. While such dogs are still warning others to stay away, they aren't interested in initiating a conflict. If left alone, they usually won't bite or attack. The body postures associated with defensive threats serve to make the dog appear smaller and less of a target. Defensively threatening dogs will show one or more fearful postures (1-6) **and** one or more threatening postures (7-10):

Figure 2. Defensively threatening
© Courtesy ASPCA.

- ❑ 1. Crouched or lowered body posture
- ❑ 2. Dog may shift body weight more to the rear quarters, as though leaning away from the opponent

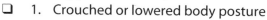

Key to My Dog's Body Postures – page 2

- ❑ 3. May move away from opponent
- ❑ 4. Ears laid back or down
- ❑ 5. Tail straight out, down, or even tucked between the legs, not wagging
- ❑ 6. Dog usually looks away from a direct stare
- ❑ 7. Teeth bared from the back of the mouth (horizontal retraction of lips)
- ❑ 8. Teeth may not be showing but muzzle may be tense and/or puckered
- ❑ 9. Snaps or tries to bite
- ❑ 10. Hackles may be up

Fearful or submissive behavior (Figures 3 and 4)

Dogs can be fearful without being threatening. Submissive and fearful behaviors overlap with each other. Dogs show submission only during social interactions, but can show fearful behaviors toward sounds and objects as well. Fearful or submissive dogs can show one or more of the following:

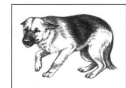

Figure 3. Submissive or fearful

- ❑ 1. Crouched body posture, or lying down, even rolled over on the back exposing the belly
- ❑ 2. May run away, or try to avoid the other person, or the fearful event or stimulus
- ❑ 3. Ears laid back or down
- ❑ 4. Tail down or tucked between the legs
- ❑ 5. Looks away and avoids direct eye contact
- ❑ 6. Eyes wide open, whites of eyes exaggerated
- ❑ 7. May retract the lips into a submissive grin
- ❑ 8. Mouth may be open but relaxed

Figure 4. Submissive

Alert or orienting behavior (Figure 5)

When something catches your dog's attention, his body posture changes from being relaxed to being focused or directed to something specific. He's not yet decided whether to be friendly, fearful or threatening–he's just paying attention. Dogs who are alerting can display one or more of the following:

Figure 5. Alert or orienting

- ❑ 1. Upright body posture, but usually not as stiff as the offensive dog–he may even be lying down
- ❑ 2. Body and gaze directed at the "thing" that has captured his attention
- ❑ 3. Ears upright

Key to My Dog's Body Postures – page 3

❑   4.   Tail variable, may be down or held high

❑   5.   Eyes open normally without a hard stare

❑   6.   Mouth open and relaxed or closed and relaxed

Friendly behavior

Surprisingly, friendly behavior is a little difficult to describe. Friendly dogs indicate a willingness to interact and they solicit attention. They may show elements of submission and play as well. Friendly dogs can show one or more of the following:

❑   1.   Body posture relaxed, not stiff-legged, may be slightly crouched or lowered

❑   2.   Moves towards the person or other dog

❑   3.   Variable ear carriage–may be upright or slightly back

❑   4.   Variable tail carriage–may be slightly lowered or held high, usually not tucked

❑   5.   If the tail is wagging, it should be a relaxed, yet rapid wag, not slow and deliberate

❑   6.   Eyes will appear "soft," without a hard stare

❑   7.   Mouth may be open or closed but is relaxed

❑   8.   May show other elements of submissive behavior

❑   9.   May lick, nudge or sniff people's hands or arms

Playful behavior (Figure 6)

Playful, friendly, and submissive behaviors often have elements in common. Dogs may show friendly behaviors in conjunction with or preceding playful behavior. Playful dogs can show one or more of the following:

❑   1.   A play bow

❑   2.   May paw at play partner

❑   3.   Variable ear carriage–may be upright or slightly back

❑   4.   Variable tail carriage–may be slightly lowered or held high, usually not tucked

❑   5.   Other friendly behaviors that alternate with threats and submissive behavior

Figure 6. Playful

© Courtesy ASPCA.

Once you have filled out the **Key to My Dog's Body Postures**, transfer this information to Question 2 of **My Dog's Barking Profile**. In general, the behavioral category with the most check marks is the one that best describes your dog's behavior when barking. If your dog appears to have several motivations at the same time, that is, you have more than one category with more than one check mark, enter all the interpretations that apply.

BarkCharts

Chart 1

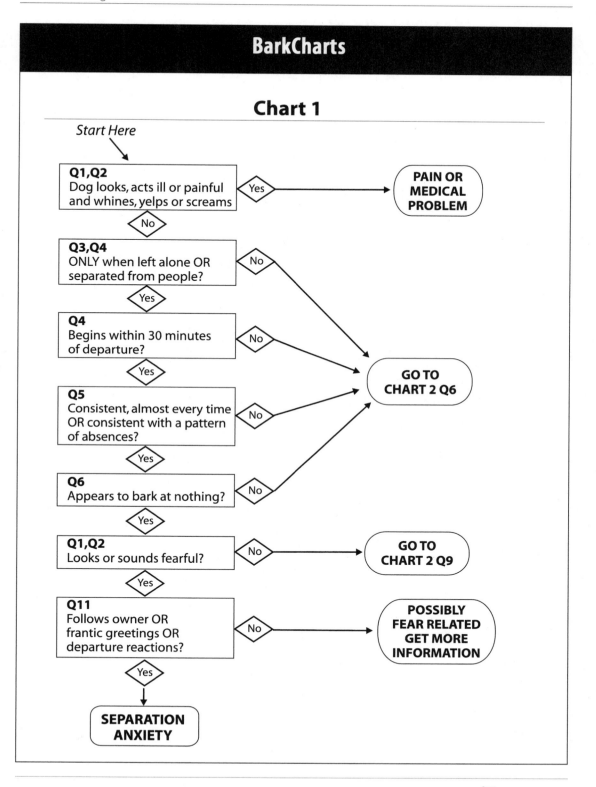

Start Here

Q1,Q2
Dog looks, acts ill or painful and whines, yelps or screams → Yes → **PAIN OR MEDICAL PROBLEM**

No

Q3,Q4
ONLY when left alone OR separated from people? → No → **GO TO CHART 2 Q6**

Yes

Q4
Begins within 30 minutes of departure? → No → **GO TO CHART 2 Q6**

Yes

Q5
Consistent, almost every time OR consistent with a pattern of absences? → No → **GO TO CHART 2 Q6**

Yes

Q6
Appears to bark at nothing? → No → **GO TO CHART 2 Q6**

Yes

Q1,Q2
Looks or sounds fearful? → No → **GO TO CHART 2 Q9**

Yes

Q11
Follows owner OR frantic greetings OR departure reactions? → No → **POSSIBLY FEAR RELATED GET MORE INFORMATION**

Yes

SEPARATION ANXIETY

BarkCharts

Chart 2

Complete Chart 1 first

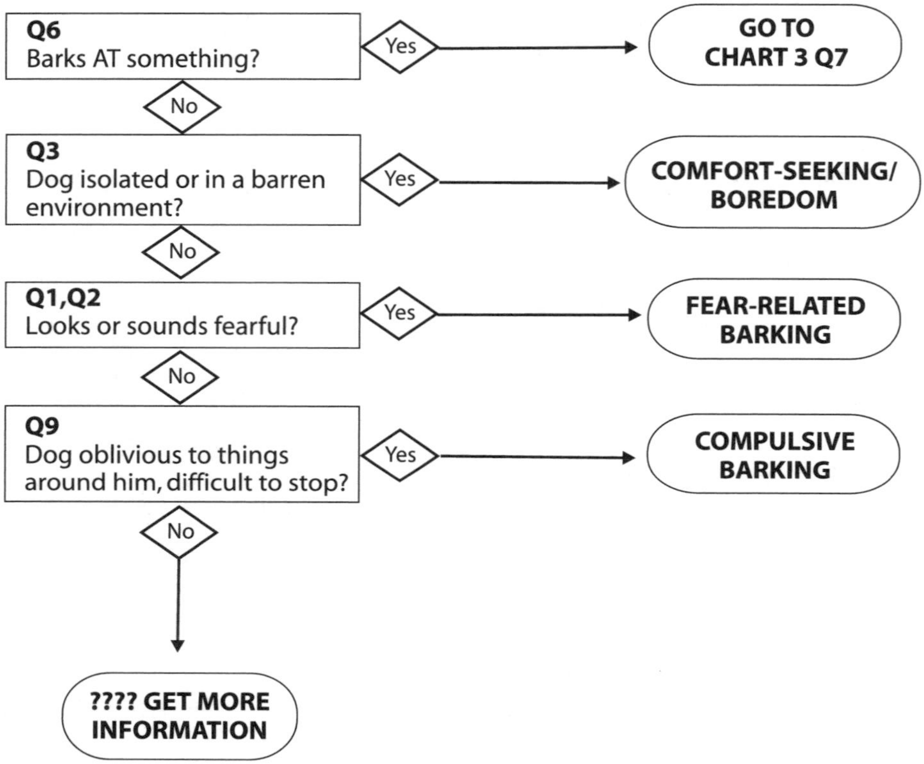

Q6
Barks AT something? — Yes → **GO TO CHART 3 Q7**

No

Q3
Dog isolated or in a barren environment? — Yes → **COMFORT-SEEKING/ BOREDOM**

No

Q1, Q2
Looks or sounds fearful? — Yes → **FEAR-RELATED BARKING**

No

Q9
Dog oblivious to things around him, difficult to stop? — Yes → **COMPULSIVE BARKING**

No

???? GET MORE INFORMATION

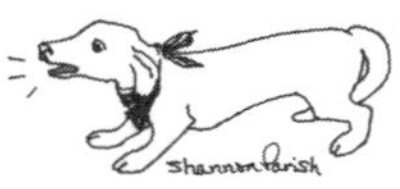

BarkCharts

Chart 3

Complete Chart 1 first

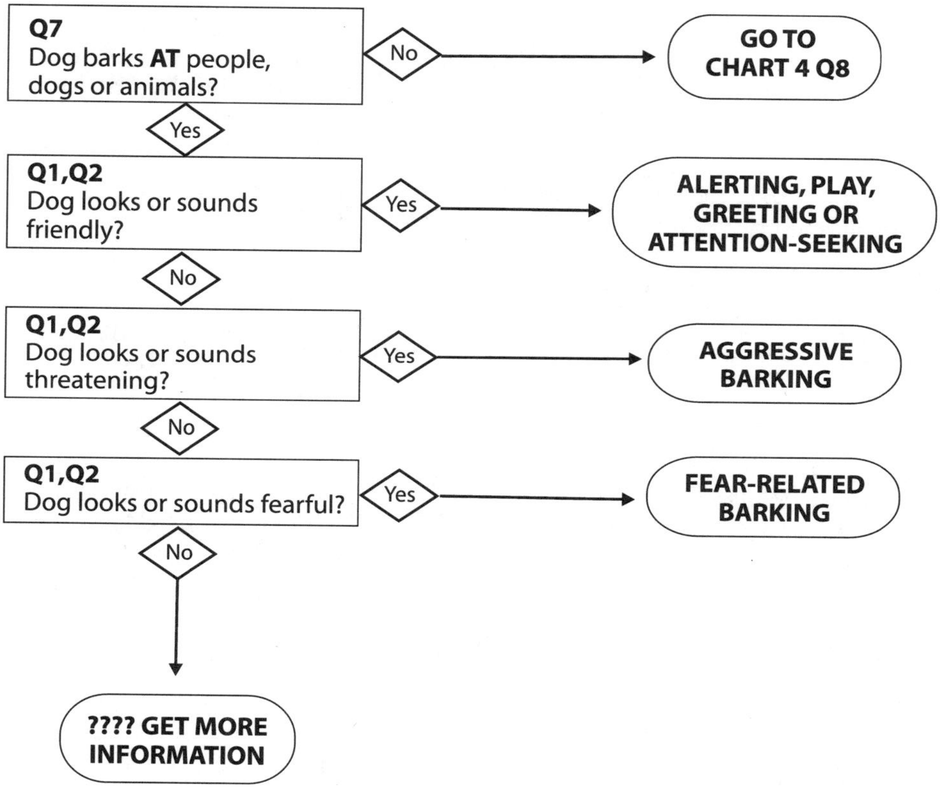

Q7
Dog barks **AT** people, dogs or animals?

No → GO TO CHART 4 Q8

Yes ↓

Q1,Q2
Dog looks or sounds friendly?

Yes → ALERTING, PLAY, GREETING OR ATTENTION-SEEKING

No ↓

Q1,Q2
Dog looks or sounds threatening?

Yes → AGGRESSIVE BARKING

No ↓

Q1,Q2
Dog looks or sounds fearful?

Yes → FEAR-RELATED BARKING

No ↓

???? GET MORE INFORMATION

Chart 4

Complete Chart 1 first

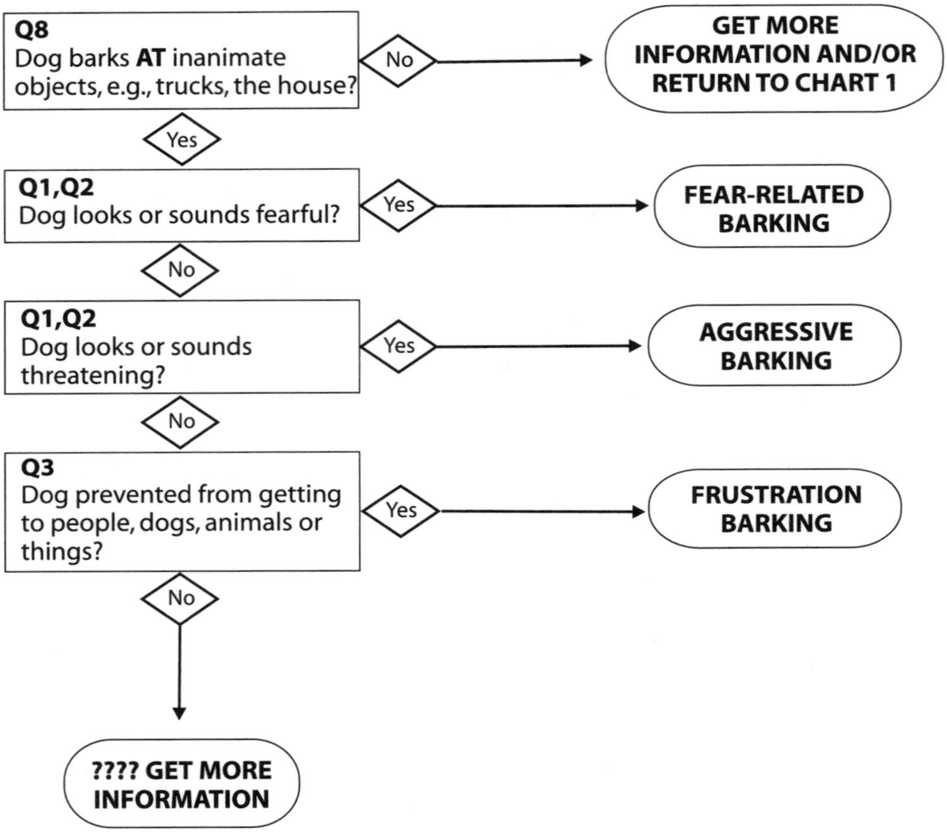

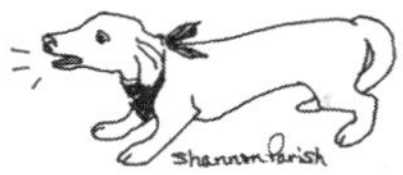

Q8
Dog barks **AT** inanimate objects, e.g., trucks, the house? — No → **GET MORE INFORMATION AND/OR RETURN TO CHART 1**

Yes ↓

Q1,Q2
Dog looks or sounds fearful? — Yes → **FEAR-RELATED BARKING**

No ↓

Q1,Q2
Dog looks or sounds threatening? — Yes → **AGGRESSIVE BARKING**

No ↓

Q3
Dog prevented from getting to people, dogs, animals or things? — Yes → **FRUSTRATION BARKING**

No ↓

???? GET MORE INFORMATION